WEIGHT WATCHERS®

1989

ENGAGEMENT CALENDAR

A PLUME BOOK

NEW AMERICAN LIBRARY

NEW YORK AND SCARBOROUGH, ONTARIO

WEIGHT WATCHERS is a registered trademark of
Weight Watchers International, Inc.

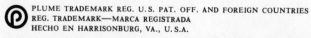
PLUME TRADEMARK REG. U.S. PAT. OFF. AND FOREIGN COUNTRIES
REG. TRADEMARK—MARCA REGISTRADA
HECHO EN HARRISONBURG, VA., U.S.A.

SIGNET, SIGNET CLASSIC, MENTOR, ONYX, PLUME, MERIDIAN and
NAL BOOKS are published *in the United States* by NAL PENGUIN INC.,
1633 Broadway, New York, New York 10019, *in Canada* by
The New American Library of Canada Limited, 81 Mack Avenue,
Scarborough, Ontario M1L 1M8

Designed by John Lynch

Cover photo by Gus Francisco

Weight Watchers is a registered trademark of
Weight Watchers International, Inc.

First Printing, August, 1988

1 2 3 4 5 6 7 8 9

PRINTED IN THE UNITED STATES OF AMERICA

It's late, you're tired, but you don't want to skip dinner. A light meal would be perfect right now. . . .

You're going out to dinner with friends, and they're stopping by first. You'd like to serve appetizers, but you're not sure what kind. . . .

You want to give the kids an after-school snack that you can also enjoy, something that won't wreck your diet. . . .

Stumped by situations like these? Don't be. Now you can enjoy luscious light meals, amazingly easy appetizers, and super snacks without going off the Food Plan. The recipes are right here in the new WEIGHT WATCHERS 1989 ENGAGEMENT CALENDAR. We've given you an assortment for each month of the year and each one of them takes just 30 minutes or less to prepare—perfect for people on the go. From light and delicious Fluffy Apple Omelet to exotic Pasta with Chicken 'n' To-matoes, you'll find great little meals that are a snap to fix. Try Open-Face Ham and Cheese Sandwiches . . . sample Shepherd's Pie . . . or go for Grilled Swordfish with Lime Butter. Looking for an even lighter bite? Refreshing Kiwi Ice, savory Pesto Toasts, and spicy Vegetable Nachos are just a few of the simple snacks and artful appetizers you'll find on these pages. And, as a special bonus, there's our Bang-Up Buffet, a year-end party with four tempting dishes that will delight both you and your guests.

Recipes aren't all you'll be delighted with, as you'll see when you leaf through this Calendar. You'll find weekly, monthly, and yearly calendar pages with plenty of room for all your appointments. There are Weekly Food Diary pages to help you keep track of the food you eat. And there's our special Meals Away from Home section with plenty of quick and easy ideas for breakfasts, coffee breaks, and lunches. Put all these features together and you just can't help being organized and efficient. And isn't that the way you want your life to be?

We do hope you enjoy using our newest WEIGHT WATCHERS ENGAGEMENT CALENDAR, and we wish you continued success in achieving your weight-loss goals.

1989

JANUARY

FEBRUARY

MAY

JUNE

SEPTEMBER

OCTOBER

1989

MARCH	APRIL
JULY	AUGUST
NOVEMBER	DECEMBER

JANUARY

SUNDAY	MONDAY	TUESDAY	WEDNESDAY
1	2	3	4
8	9	10	11
15	16	17	18
22	23	24	25
29	30	31	

JANUARY

THURSDAY	FRIDAY	SATURDAY	NOTES/GOALS
5	6	7	
12	13	14	
19	20	21	
26	27	28	

WEEKLY FOOD DIARY

	MONDAY	TUESDAY	WEDNESDAY	THURSDAY	FRIDAY	SATURDAY	SUNDAY
BREAKFAST							
LUNCH							
DINNER							
SNACKS							
DAILY TOTALS	FRUIT ___ VEG ___ FAT ___ PROTEIN ___ BREAD ___ MILK ___ FLOATING ___	FRUIT ___ VEG ___ FAT ___ PROTEIN ___ BREAD ___ MILK ___ FLOATING ___	FRUIT ___ VEG ___ FAT ___ PROTEIN ___ BREAD ___ MILK ___ FLOATING ___	FRUIT ___ VEG ___ FAT ___ PROTEIN ___ BREAD ___ MILK ___ FLOATING ___	FRUIT ___ VEG ___ FAT ___ PROTEIN ___ BREAD ___ MILK ___ FLOATING ___	FRUIT ___ VEG ___ FAT ___ PROTEIN ___ BREAD ___ MILK ___ FLOATING ___	FRUIT ___ VEG ___ FAT ___ PROTEIN ___ BREAD ___ MILK ___ FLOATING ___

WEEKLY LIMITS   EGGS ___   CHEESE ___   MEAT ___   ORGAN MEAT ___   OPTIONAL CALORIES ___

I will attend my Weight Watchers meeting this week on ___

ENGAGEMENTS

DECEMBER
JANUARY

1 9 8 9

MONDAY
26

TUESDAY
27

WEDNESDAY
28

THURSDAY
29

FRIDAY
30

New Year's Eve 1988

SATURDAY
31

New Year's Day 1989

SUNDAY
1

	S	M	T	W	T	F	S
					1	2	3
D	4	5	6	7	8	9	10
E	11	12	13	14	15	16	17
C	18	19	20	21	22	23	24
	25	26	27	28	29	30	31

	S	M	T	W	T	F	S
	1	2	3	4	5	6	7
J	8	9	10	11	12	13	14
A	15	16	17	18	19	20	21
N	22	23	24	25	26	27	28
	29	30	31				

	S	M	T	W	T	F	S
				1	2	3	4
F	5	6	7	8	9	10	11
E	12	13	14	15	16	17	18
B	19	20	21	22	23	24	25
	26	27	28				

WEEKLY FOOD DIARY

	MONDAY	TUESDAY	WEDNESDAY	THURSDAY	FRIDAY	SATURDAY	SUNDAY
BREAKFAST							
LUNCH							
DINNER							
SNACKS							
DAILY TOTALS	FRUIT ___ VEG ___ FAT ___ PROTEIN ___ BREAD ___ MILK ___ FLOATING ___	FRUIT ___ VEG ___ FAT ___ PROTEIN ___ BREAD ___ MILK ___ FLOATING ___	FRUIT ___ VEG ___ FAT ___ PROTEIN ___ BREAD ___ MILK ___ FLOATING ___	FRUIT ___ VEG ___ FAT ___ PROTEIN ___ BREAD ___ MILK ___ FLOATING ___	FRUIT ___ VEG ___ FAT ___ PROTEIN ___ BREAD ___ MILK ___ FLOATING ___	FRUIT ___ VEG ___ FAT ___ PROTEIN ___ BREAD ___ MILK ___ FLOATING ___	FRUIT ___ VEG ___ FAT ___ PROTEIN ___ BREAD ___ MILK ___ FLOATING ___

WEEKLY LIMITS   EGGS _____   CHEESE _____   MEAT _____   ORGAN MEAT _____   OPTIONAL CALORIES _____

I will attend my Weight Watchers meeting this week on _____

E N G A G E M E N T S

JANUARY

1 9 8 9

MONDAY
2

TUESDAY
3

WEDNESDAY
4

THURSDAY
5

FRIDAY
6

SATURDAY
7

SUNDAY
8

	S	M	T	W	T	F	S
					1	2	3
D	4	5	6	7	8	9	10
E	11	12	13	14	15	16	17
C	18	19	20	21	22	23	24
	25	26	27	28	29	30	31

	S	M	T	W	T	F	S
	1	2	3	4	5	6	7
	8	9	10	11	12	13	14
J	15	16	17	18	19	20	21
A	22	23	24	25	26	27	28
N	29	30	31				

	S	M	T	W	T	F	S
				1	2	3	4
	5	6	7	8	9	10	11
F	12	13	14	15	16	17	18
E	19	20	21	22	23	24	25
B	26	27	28				

WEEKLY FOOD DIARY

	MONDAY	TUESDAY	WEDNESDAY	THURSDAY	FRIDAY	SATURDAY	SUNDAY
BREAKFAST							
LUNCH							
DINNER							
SNACKS							
DAILY TOTALS	FRUIT ___ VEG ___ FAT ___ PROTEIN ___ BREAD ___ MILK ___ FLOATING ___	FRUIT ___ VEG ___ FAT ___ PROTEIN ___ BREAD ___ MILK ___ FLOATING ___	FRUIT ___ VEG ___ FAT ___ PROTEIN ___ BREAD ___ MILK ___ FLOATING ___	FRUIT ___ VEG ___ FAT ___ PROTEIN ___ BREAD ___ MILK ___ FLOATING ___	FRUIT ___ VEG ___ FAT ___ PROTEIN ___ BREAD ___ MILK ___ FLOATING ___	FRUIT ___ VEG ___ FAT ___ PROTEIN ___ BREAD ___ MILK ___ FLOATING ___	FRUIT ___ VEG ___ FAT ___ PROTEIN ___ BREAD ___ MILK ___ FLOATING ___

WEEKLY LIMITS EGGS _____ CHEESE _____ MEAT _____ ORGAN MEAT _____ OPTIONAL CALORIES _____

I will attend my Weight Watchers meeting this week on _____

MONDAY
9

TUESDAY
10

WEDNESDAY
11

THURSDAY
12

FRIDAY
13

SATURDAY
14

Martin Luther King, Jr.'s Birthday

SUNDAY
15

	S	M	T	W	T	F	S
						1	2	3
D	4	5	6	7	8	9	10
E	11	12	13	14	15	16	17
C	18	19	20	21	22	23	24
	25	26	27	28	29	30	31

	S	M	T	W	T	F	S
	1	2	3	4	5	6	7
J	8	9	10	11	12	13	14
A	15	16	17	18	19	20	21
N	22	23	24	25	26	27	28
	29	30	31				

	S	M	T	W	T	F	S
				1	2	3	4
F	5	6	7	8	9	10	11
E	12	13	14	15	16	17	18
B	19	20	21	22	23	24	25
	26	27	28				

WEEKLY FOOD DIARY

	MONDAY	TUESDAY	WEDNESDAY	THURSDAY	FRIDAY	SATURDAY	SUNDAY
BREAKFAST							
LUNCH							
DINNER							
SNACKS							
DAILY TOTALS	FRUIT ___ VEG ___ FAT ___ PROTEIN ___ BREAD ___ MILK ___ FLOATING ___	FRUIT ___ VEG ___ FAT ___ PROTEIN ___ BREAD ___ MILK ___ FLOATING ___	FRUIT ___ VEG ___ FAT ___ PROTEIN ___ BREAD ___ MILK ___ FLOATING ___	FRUIT ___ VEG ___ FAT ___ PROTEIN ___ BREAD ___ MILK ___ FLOATING ___	FRUIT ___ VEG ___ FAT ___ PROTEIN ___ BREAD ___ MILK ___ FLOATING ___	FRUIT ___ VEG ___ FAT ___ PROTEIN ___ BREAD ___ MILK ___ FLOATING ___	FRUIT ___ VEG ___ FAT ___ PROTEIN ___ BREAD ___ MILK ___ FLOATING ___

WEEKLY LIMITS   EGGS _____   CHEESE _____   MEAT _____   ORGAN MEAT _____   OPTIONAL CALORIES _____

I will attend my Weight Watchers meeting this week on _____

JANUARY

1 9 8 9

Martin Luther King, Jr.'s Birthday
(observed)

MONDAY
16

TUESDAY
17

WEDNESDAY
18

THURSDAY
19

FRIDAY
20

SATURDAY
21

SUNDAY
22

	S	M	T	W	T	F	S
						1	2	3
D	4	5	6	7	8	9	10
E	11	12	13	14	15	16	17
C	18	19	20	21	22	23	24
	25	26	27	28	29	30	31

	S	M	T	W	T	F	S
	1	2	3	4	5	6	7
J	8	9	10	11	12	13	14
A	15	16	17	18	19	20	21
N	22	23	24	25	26	27	28
	29	30	31				

	S	M	T	W	T	F	S
				1	2	3	4
F	5	6	7	8	9	10	11
E	12	13	14	15	16	17	18
B	19	20	21	22	23	24	25
	26	27	28				

WEEKLY FOOD DIARY

	MONDAY	TUESDAY	WEDNESDAY	THURSDAY	FRIDAY	SATURDAY	SUNDAY
BREAKFAST							
LUNCH							
DINNER							
SNACKS							
DAILY TOTALS	FRUIT ___ VEG ___ FAT ___ PROTEIN ___ BREAD ___ MILK ___ FLOATING ___	FRUIT ___ VEG ___ FAT ___ PROTEIN ___ BREAD ___ MILK ___ FLOATING ___	FRUIT ___ VEG ___ FAT ___ PROTEIN ___ BREAD ___ MILK ___ FLOATING ___	FRUIT ___ VEG ___ FAT ___ PROTEIN ___ BREAD ___ MILK ___ FLOATING ___	FRUIT ___ VEG ___ FAT ___ PROTEIN ___ BREAD ___ MILK ___ FLOATING ___	FRUIT ___ VEG ___ FAT ___ PROTEIN ___ BREAD ___ MILK ___ FLOATING ___	FRUIT ___ VEG ___ FAT ___ PROTEIN ___ BREAD ___ MILK ___ FLOATING ___

WEEKLY LIMITS   EGGS _____   CHEESE _____   MEAT _____   ORGAN MEAT _____   OPTIONAL CALORIES _____

I will attend my Weight Watchers meeting this week on _____

ENGAGEMENTS

JANUARY

1 9 8 9

MONDAY
23

TUESDAY
24

WEDNESDAY
25

THURSDAY
26

FRIDAY
27

SATURDAY
28

SUNDAY
29

	S	M	T	W	T	F	S
						1	2	3
D	4	5	6	7	8	9	10
E	11	12	13	14	15	16	17
C	18	19	20	21	22	23	24
	25	26	27	28	29	30	31

	S	M	T	W	T	F	S
	1	2	3	4	5	6	7
J	8	9	10	11	12	13	14
A	15	16	17	18	19	20	21
N	22	23	24	25	26	27	28
	29	30	31				

	S	M	T	W	T	F	S
				1	2	3	4
F	5	6	7	8	9	10	11
E	12	13	14	15	16	17	18
B	19	20	21	22	23	24	25
	26	27	28				

Potato Skins with Bacon and Cheddar

Makes 2 servings, 4 filled potato skins each

This popular appetizer has been appearing more and more on restaurant menus. Now you can make it at home.

1 baked potato (9 ounces)
2 teaspoons vegetable oil
2 slices crisp bacon, crumbled

2 ounces Cheddar cheese, shredded
Garnish: 2 teaspoons chopped fresh parsley

Cut potato in half lengthwise and, using a spoon, scoop out pulp from each half, leaving two ¼- to ⅛-inch-thick shells (each potato shell should weigh 3 ounces).* Cut each potato shell lengthwise into quarters and place each shell quarter skin-side down on nonstick baking sheet. Using a pastry brush, lightly brush ¼ teaspoon oil evenly over pulp side of each shell quarter; broil until lightly browned, 2 to 3 minutes. Fill each shell quarter with ⅛ of the bacon, then sprinkle with ⅛ of the cheese. Broil until cheese melts, 1 to 2 minutes. Serve garnished with parsley.

Each serving provides: 1 Protein Exchange; 1 Bread Exchange; 1 Fat Exchange; 45 Optional Calories

Per serving: 284 calories; 11 g protein; 17 g fat; 22 g carbohydrate; 214 mg calcium; 284 mg sodium; 35 mg cholesterol; 2 g dietary fiber

* Reserve potato pulp and store in resealable plastic container; refrigerate for use at another time.

Linguine and Clams

Makes 2 servings

Start an Italian dinner with this traditional dish, or enjoy it as a light and hearty lunch.

2 teaspoons olive oil
¼ cup chopped onion
2 garlic cloves, minced
12 small littleneck clams,* scrubbed
1 medium tomato, blanched, peeled,
   seeded, and chopped
¼ cup *each* bottled clam juice and dry
   white table wine

1 tablespoon chopped fresh parsley
¼ teaspoon thyme leaves
Dash pepper
1 cup cooked linguine (hot)
2 tablespoons grated Parmesan cheese

In 10-inch nonstick skillet heat oil; add onion and garlic and sauté over high heat, stirring frequently, until softened, about 1 minute. Add remaining ingredients except linguine and cheese; cover and cook until clam shells open, 4 to 5 minutes.

To serve, arrange linguine in serving bowl; top with clam mixture and sprinkle with Parmesan cheese.

Each serving provides: 1 Protein Exchange; 1 Bread Exchange; 1¼ Vegetable Exchanges; 1 Fat Exchange; 65 Optional Calories

Per serving: 232 calories; 13 g protein; 7 g fat; 24 g carbohydrate; 124 mg calcium; 254 mg sodium; 26 mg cholesterol; 1 g dietary fiber

* 12 small littleneck clams will yield about 2 ounces cooked clam meat.

WEIGHT RECIPE WATCHERS

Sausage Bites

Makes 2 servings

You and your guests will savor the wonderful combination of flavors in this quick and easy hors d'oeuvre.

2 tablespoons *each* minced scallion (green onion) and dry red table wine
1 tablespoon Dijon-style mustard

Dash *each* ground allspice and pepper
2 ounces precooked smoked beef sausage, cut crosswise into ¼-inch-thick slices

In small saucepan combine all ingredients except sausage and cook over medium-low heat, stirring occasionally, until bubbly, 1 to 2 minutes. Stir in sausage slices and cook, stirring occasionally, until heated through, about 5 minutes.

Each serving provides: 1 Protein Exchange; ⅛ Vegetable Exchange; 15 Optional Calories

Per serving: 115 calories; 4 g protein; 9 g fat; 3 g carbohydrate; 6 mg calcium; 502 mg sodium; 8 mg cholesterol; 0.1 g dietary fiber

Greek Snack Slices

Makes 2 servings

1 ounce feta cheese, crumbled
3 tablespoons whipped cream cheese
1 tablespoon *each* minced scallion
  (green onion), radish, and fresh dill
2 pitted black olives, minced

1 teaspoon lemon juice
Dash garlic powder
1 large cucumber (about 9½ ounces),
  cut into eight 1-inch-thick slices
Garnish: dill sprigs

Using a fork, in small mixing bowl combine all ingredients except cucumber and garnish, mixing until blended. Spoon an equal amount of cheese mixture onto center of each cucumber slice. Arrange cucumber slices on serving platter and garnish each slice with a dill sprig.

Each serving provides: ½ Protein Exchange; 1¼ Vegetable Exchanges; 55 Optional Calories

Per serving: 114 calories; 4 g protein; 9 g fat; 6 g carbohydrate; 114 mg calcium; 232 mg sodium; 28 mg cholesterol; 0.8 g dietary fiber

FEBRUARY

SUNDAY	MONDAY	TUESDAY	WEDNESDAY
			1
5	6	7	8
12	13	14	15
19	20	21	22
26	27	28	

FEBRUARY

THURSDAY	FRIDAY	SATURDAY	NOTES/GOALS
2	3	4	
9	10	11	
16	17	18	
23	24	25	

WEEKLY FOOD DIARY

	MONDAY	TUESDAY	WEDNESDAY	THURSDAY	FRIDAY	SATURDAY	SUNDAY
BREAKFAST							
LUNCH							
DINNER							
SNACKS							
DAILY TOTALS	FRUIT _____ VEG _____ FAT _____ PROTEIN _____ BREAD _____ MILK _____ FLOATING _____	FRUIT _____ VEG _____ FAT _____ PROTEIN _____ BREAD _____ MILK _____ FLOATING _____	FRUIT _____ VEG _____ FAT _____ PROTEIN _____ BREAD _____ MILK _____ FLOATING _____	FRUIT _____ VEG _____ FAT _____ PROTEIN _____ BREAD _____ MILK _____ FLOATING _____	FRUIT _____ VEG _____ FAT _____ PROTEIN _____ BREAD _____ MILK _____ FLOATING _____	FRUIT _____ VEG _____ FAT _____ PROTEIN _____ BREAD _____ MILK _____ FLOATING _____	FRUIT _____ VEG _____ FAT _____ PROTEIN _____ BREAD _____ MILK _____ FLOATING _____

WEEKLY LIMITS   EGGS _____   CHEESE _____   MEAT _____   ORGAN MEAT _____   OPTIONAL CALORIES _____

I will attend my Weight Watchers meeting this week on _____

MONDAY
30

TUESDAY
31

WEDNESDAY
1

THURSDAY
2

FRIDAY
3

SATURDAY
4

SUNDAY
5

	S	M	T	W	T	F	S
	1	2	3	4	5	6	7
J	8	9	10	11	12	13	14
A	15	16	17	18	19	20	21
N	22	23	24	25	26	27	28
	29	30	31				

	S	M	T	W	T	F	S
				1	2	3	4
F	5	6	7	8	9	10	11
E	12	13	14	15	16	17	18
B	19	20	21	22	23	24	25
	26	27	28				

	S	M	T	W	T	F	S
				1	2	3	4
M	5	6	7	8	9	10	11
A	12	13	14	15	16	17	18
R	19	20	21	22	23	24	25
	26	27	28	29	30	31	

WEEKLY FOOD DIARY

	MONDAY	TUESDAY	WEDNESDAY	THURSDAY	FRIDAY	SATURDAY	SUNDAY
BREAKFAST							
LUNCH							
DINNER							
SNACKS							
DAILY TOTALS	FRUIT ___ VEG ___ FAT ___ PROTEIN ___ BREAD ___ MILK ___ FLOATING ___	FRUIT ___ VEG ___ FAT ___ PROTEIN ___ BREAD ___ MILK ___ FLOATING ___	FRUIT ___ VEG ___ FAT ___ PROTEIN ___ BREAD ___ MILK ___ FLOATING ___	FRUIT ___ VEG ___ FAT ___ PROTEIN ___ BREAD ___ MILK ___ FLOATING ___	FRUIT ___ VEG ___ FAT ___ PROTEIN ___ BREAD ___ MILK ___ FLOATING ___	FRUIT ___ VEG ___ FAT ___ PROTEIN ___ BREAD ___ MILK ___ FLOATING ___	FRUIT ___ VEG ___ FAT ___ PROTEIN ___ BREAD ___ MILK ___ FLOATING ___

WEEKLY LIMITS   EGGS ___   CHEESE ___   MEAT ___   ORGAN MEAT ___   OPTIONAL CALORIES ___

I will attend my Weight Watchers meeting this week on ___

MONDAY
6

TUESDAY
7

Ash Wednesday

WEDNESDAY
8

THURSDAY
9

FRIDAY
10

SATURDAY
11

Lincoln's Birthday

SUNDAY
12

	S	M	T	W	T	F	S
		1	2	3	4	5	6	7
J	8	9	10	11	12	13	14
A	15	16	17	18	19	20	21
N	22	23	24	25	26	27	28
	29	30	31				

	S	M	T	W	T	F	S
				1	2	3	4
F	5	6	7	8	9	10	11
E	12	13	14	15	16	17	18
B	19	20	21	22	23	24	25
	26	27	28				

	S	M	T	W	T	F	S
				1	2	3	4
M	5	6	7	8	9	10	11
A	12	13	14	15	16	17	18
R	19	20	21	22	23	24	25
	26	27	28	29	30	31	

WEEKLY FOOD DIARY

	MONDAY	TUESDAY	WEDNESDAY	THURSDAY	FRIDAY	SATURDAY	SUNDAY
BREAKFAST							
LUNCH							
DINNER							
SNACKS							
DAILY TOTALS	FRUIT ___ VEG ___ FAT ___ PROTEIN ___ BREAD ___ MILK ___ FLOATING ___	FRUIT ___ VEG ___ FAT ___ PROTEIN ___ BREAD ___ MILK ___ FLOATING ___	FRUIT ___ VEG ___ FAT ___ PROTEIN ___ BREAD ___ MILK ___ FLOATING ___	FRUIT ___ VEG ___ FAT ___ PROTEIN ___ BREAD ___ MILK ___ FLOATING ___	FRUIT ___ VEG ___ FAT ___ PROTEIN ___ BREAD ___ MILK ___ FLOATING ___	FRUIT ___ VEG ___ FAT ___ PROTEIN ___ BREAD ___ MILK ___ FLOATING ___	FRUIT ___ VEG ___ FAT ___ PROTEIN ___ BREAD ___ MILK ___ FLOATING ___

WEEKLY LIMITS EGGS _____ CHEESE _____ MEAT _____ ORGAN MEAT _____ OPTIONAL CALORIES _____

I will attend my Weight Watchers meeting this week on _____

MONDAY
13

Valentine's Day

TUESDAY
14

WEDNESDAY
15

THURSDAY
16

FRIDAY
17

SATURDAY
18

SUNDAY
19

	S	M	T	W	T	F	S
		1	2	3	4	5	6	7
J	8	9	10	11	12	13	14
A	15	16	17	18	19	20	21
N	22	23	24	25	26	27	28
	29	30	31

	S	M	T	W	T	F	S
				1	2	3	4
F	5	6	7	8	9	10	11
E	12	13	14	15	16	17	18
B	19	20	21	22	23	24	25
	26	27	28

	S	M	T	W	T	F	S
				1	2	3	4
M	5	6	7	8	9	10	11
A	12	13	14	15	16	17	18
R	19	20	21	22	23	24	25
	26	27	28	29	30	31

WEEKLY FOOD DIARY

	MONDAY	TUESDAY	WEDNESDAY	THURSDAY	FRIDAY	SATURDAY	SUNDAY
BREAKFAST							
LUNCH							
DINNER							
SNACKS							
DAILY TOTALS	FRUIT ___ VEG ___ FAT ___ PROTEIN ___ BREAD ___ MILK ___ FLOATING ___	FRUIT ___ VEG ___ FAT ___ PROTEIN ___ BREAD ___ MILK ___ FLOATING ___	FRUIT ___ VEG ___ FAT ___ PROTEIN ___ BREAD ___ MILK ___ FLOATING ___	FRUIT ___ VEG ___ FAT ___ PROTEIN ___ BREAD ___ MILK ___ FLOATING ___	FRUIT ___ VEG ___ FAT ___ PROTEIN ___ BREAD ___ MILK ___ FLOATING ___	FRUIT ___ VEG ___ FAT ___ PROTEIN ___ BREAD ___ MILK ___ FLOATING ___	FRUIT ___ VEG ___ FAT ___ PROTEIN ___ BREAD ___ MILK ___ FLOATING ___

WEEKLY LIMITS EGGS _____   CHEESE _____   MEAT _____   ORGAN MEAT _____   OPTIONAL CALORIES _____

I will attend my Weight Watchers meeting this week on _____

FEBRUARY

1 9 8 9

Washington's Birthday (observed)

MONDAY
20

TUESDAY
21

Washington's Birthday

WEDNESDAY
22

THURSDAY
23

FRIDAY
24

SATURDAY
25

SUNDAY
26

	S	M	T	W	T	F	S
	1	2	3	4	5	6	7
J	8	9	10	11	12	13	14
A	15	16	17	18	19	20	21
N	22	23	24	25	26	27	28
	29	30	31				

	S	M	T	W	T	F	S
				1	2	3	4
F	5	6	7	8	9	10	11
E	12	13	14	15	16	17	18
B	19	20	21	22	23	24	25
	26	27	28				

	S	M	T	W	T	F	S
				1	2	3	4
M	5	6	7	8	9	10	11
A	12	13	14	15	16	17	18
R	19	20	21	22	23	24	25
	26	27	28	29	30	31	

Spicy Lasagna Chips

Makes 4 servings, 4 chips each

This crunchy snack is an unusual and delicious change of pace from ordinary chips.

4 uncooked curly-edge lasagna noodles (¾ ounce each), cooked according to package directions and drained

2 teaspoons *each* water and olive *or* vegetable oil

1 teaspoon *each* basil leaves and oregano leaves

½ teaspoon *each* onion powder and garlic powder

Dash ground red pepper

1 tablespoon plus 1 teaspoon grated Parmesan cheese

Preheat oven to 400°F. Using paper towels pat noodles dry. Cut each noodle crosswise into four equal pieces. In cup or small bowl combine water and oil; using a pastry brush, brush both sides of each piece of noodle with an equal amount of oil mixture and arrange in a single layer on nonstick baking sheet. In clean dry cup or small bowl combine seasonings and sprinkle evenly over noodles, then sprinkle evenly with cheese. Bake until crisp and browned, 12 to 15 minutes; let cool on wire rack. Store in airtight container until ready to serve.

Each serving provides: 1 Bread Exchange; ½ Fat Exchange; 10 Optional Calories

Per serving: 110 calories; 4 g protein; 3 g fat; 17 g carbohydrate; 44 mg calcium; 32 mg sodium; 1 mg cholesterol; 0.5 g dietary fiber

Open-Face Ham and Cheese Sandwiches

Makes 2 servings

1 whole-wheat English muffin, split in half and toasted

2 teaspoons Dijon-style *or* regular prepared mustard

2 ounces Brie cheese (at room temperature), cut into 4 equal pieces

2 ounces thinly sliced baked Virginia ham

4 thin tomato slices

Preheat oven to 350°F. On baking sheet set each muffin half split-side up and spread with 1 teaspoon mustard. Top each half with 1 piece of cheese, then 1 ounce ham and 2 tomato slices; top each portion of tomato with 1 remaining piece of cheese. Bake until cheese melts, about 5 minutes.*

Each serving provides: 2 Protein Exchanges; 1 Bread Exchange; ½ Vegetable Exchange

Per serving: 211 calories; 14 g protein; 10 g fat; 16 g carbohydrate; 56 mg calcium; 784 mg sodium; 43 mg cholesterol; 3 g dietary fiber

* If crisper topping is desired, after baking broil until cheese is golden brown, about 2 minutes.

Sweet Trail Mix

Makes 2 servings

¼ **ounce** *each* **semisweet mini chocolate chips and pignolia nuts (pine nuts), toasted**
2 tablespoons golden raisins

1 tablespoon dried currants*
2 dried apricot halves, finely chopped
2 teaspoons shredded coconut

In small mixing bowl combine all ingredients. Store in airtight container until ready to serve.

Each serving provides: 1 Fruit Exchange; 55 Optional Calories

Per serving: 92 calories; 2 g protein; 4 g fat; 16 g carbohydrate; 12 mg calcium; 6 mg sodium; 0 mg cholesterol; dietary fiber data not available

* 1 tablespoon dark raisins may be substituted for the currants.

Chimichangas (Fried Filled Tortillas)

Makes 2 servings, 2 filled tortillas each

Our version of this Mexican favorite makes a wonderfully satisfying light meal or a great beginning to a Mexican fiesta.

4 flour tortillas (6-inch diameter each)
4 ounces drained canned pink beans, mashed
2 ounces Monterery Jack cheese, shredded
½ medium tomato, seeded and diced
⅛ avocado (1 ounce), pared and diced

1 tablespoon *each* diced red bell pepper and scallion (green onion)
1½ teaspoons *each* minced cilantro (Chinese parsley), optional, and seeded and minced hot chili pepper
½ small garlic clove, mashed
1 tablespoon vegetable oil

Preheat oven to 350°F. Arrange tortillas in a stack; wrap in foil and bake until more flexible, 10 to 15 minutes. In small mixing bowl combine all ingredients except tortillas and oil. Set 1 tortilla on work surface. Spoon ¼ of filling (about ¼ cup) onto lower third of tortilla, leaving a 1-inch edge on bottom and sides. Fold lower edge up over filling, then fold in sides of tortilla. Roll filled tortilla up toward top edge to enclose; secure with a toothpick. Repeat procedure, using remaining tortillas and filling.

In 10-inch skillet heat oil over medium-high heat; carefully add tortillas and cook, turning once, until browned on all sides, about 5 minutes on each side.

Each serving provides: 2 Protein Exchanges; 2 Bread Exchanges; ¾ Vegetable Exchange; 1½ Fat Exchanges; 25 Optional Calories

Per serving: 407 calories; 16 g protein; 21 g fat; 41 g carbohydrate; 329 mg calcium; 618 mg sodium; 25 mg cholesterol; 6 g dietary fiber

MARCH

SUNDAY	MONDAY	TUESDAY	WEDNESDAY
			1
5	6	7	8
12	13	14	15
19	20	21	22
26	27	28	29

MARCH

THURSDAY	FRIDAY	SATURDAY	NOTES/GOALS
2	3	4	
9	10	11	
16	17	18	
23	24	25	
30	31		

WEEKLY FOOD DIARY

	MONDAY	TUESDAY	WEDNESDAY	THURSDAY	FRIDAY	SATURDAY	SUNDAY
BREAKFAST							
LUNCH							
DINNER							
SNACKS							
DAILY TOTALS	FRUIT ___ VEG ___ FAT ___ PROTEIN ___ BREAD ___ MILK ___ FLOATING ___	FRUIT ___ VEG ___ FAT ___ PROTEIN ___ BREAD ___ MILK ___ FLOATING ___	FRUIT ___ VEG ___ FAT ___ PROTEIN ___ BREAD ___ MILK ___ FLOATING ___	FRUIT ___ VEG ___ FAT ___ PROTEIN ___ BREAD ___ MILK ___ FLOATING ___	FRUIT ___ VEG ___ FAT ___ PROTEIN ___ BREAD ___ MILK ___ FLOATING ___	FRUIT ___ VEG ___ FAT ___ PROTEIN ___ BREAD ___ MILK ___ FLOATING ___	FRUIT ___ VEG ___ FAT ___ PROTEIN ___ BREAD ___ MILK ___ FLOATING ___

WEEKLY LIMITS   EGGS _____   CHEESE _____   MEAT _____   ORGAN MEAT _____   OPTIONAL CALORIES _____

I will attend my Weight Watchers meeting this week on _____

FEBRUARY
MARCH

1 9 8 9

MONDAY
27

TUESDAY
28

WEDNESDAY
1

THURSDAY
2

FRIDAY
3

SATURDAY
4

SUNDAY
5

	S	M	T	W	T	F	S
				1	2	3	4
F	5	6	7	8	9	10	11
E	12	13	14	15	16	17	18
B	19	20	21	22	23	24	25
	26	27	28				

	S	M	T	W	T	F	S
				1	2	3	4
M	5	6	7	8	9	10	11
A	12	13	14	15	16	17	18
R	19	20	21	22	23	24	25
	26	27	28	29	30	31	

	S	M	T	W	T	F	S
							1
A	2	3	4	5	6	7	8
P	9	10	11	12	13	14	15
R	16	17	18	19	20	21	22
	23	24	25	26	27	28	29
	30						

WEEKLY FOOD DIARY

	MONDAY	TUESDAY	WEDNESDAY	THURSDAY	FRIDAY	SATURDAY	SUNDAY
BREAKFAST							
LUNCH							
DINNER							
SNACKS							
DAILY TOTALS	FRUIT _____ VEG _____ FAT _____ PROTEIN _____ BREAD _____ MILK _____ FLOATING _____	FRUIT _____ VEG _____ FAT _____ PROTEIN _____ BREAD _____ MILK _____ FLOATING _____	FRUIT _____ VEG _____ FAT _____ PROTEIN _____ BREAD _____ MILK _____ FLOATING _____	FRUIT _____ VEG _____ FAT _____ PROTEIN _____ BREAD _____ MILK _____ FLOATING _____	FRUIT _____ VEG _____ FAT _____ PROTEIN _____ BREAD _____ MILK _____ FLOATING _____	FRUIT _____ VEG _____ FAT _____ PROTEIN _____ BREAD _____ MILK _____ FLOATING _____

WEEKLY LIMITS   EGGS _____   CHEESE _____   MEAT _____   ORGAN MEAT _____   OPTIONAL CALORIES _____

I will attend my Weight Watchers meeting this week on _____

ENGAGEMENTS

MARCH

1989

MONDAY
6

TUESDAY
7

WEDNESDAY
8

THURSDAY
9

FRIDAY
10

SATURDAY
11

SUNDAY
12

	S	M	T	W	T	F	S
				1	2	3	4
F	5	6	7	8	9	10	11
E	12	13	14	15	16	17	18
B	19	20	21	22	23	24	25
	26	27	28				

	S	M	T	W	T	F	S
				1	2	3	4
M	5	6	7	8	9	10	11
A	12	13	14	15	16	17	18
R	19	20	21	22	23	24	25
	26	27	28	29	30	31	

	S	M	T	W	T	F	S
							1
A	2	3	4	5	6	7	8
P	9	10	11	12	13	14	15
R	16	17	18	19	20	21	22
	23	24	25	26	27	28	29
	30						

WEEKLY FOOD DIARY

	MONDAY	TUESDAY	WEDNESDAY	THURSDAY	FRIDAY	SATURDAY	SUNDAY
BREAKFAST							
LUNCH							
DINNER							
SNACKS							
DAILY TOTALS	FRUIT ___ VEG ___ FAT ___ PROTEIN ___ BREAD ___ MILK ___ FLOATING ___	FRUIT ___ VEG ___ FAT ___ PROTEIN ___ BREAD ___ MILK ___ FLOATING ___	FRUIT ___ VEG ___ FAT ___ PROTEIN ___ BREAD ___ MILK ___ FLOATING ___	FRUIT ___ VEG ___ FAT ___ PROTEIN ___ BREAD ___ MILK ___ FLOATING ___	FRUIT ___ VEG ___ FAT ___ PROTEIN ___ BREAD ___ MILK ___ FLOATING ___	FRUIT ___ VEG ___ FAT ___ PROTEIN ___ BREAD ___ MILK ___ FLOATING ___	FRUIT ___ VEG ___ FAT ___ PROTEIN ___ BREAD ___ MILK ___ FLOATING ___

WEEKLY LIMITS EGGS _____ CHEESE _____ MEAT _____ ORGAN MEAT _____ OPTIONAL CALORIES _____

I will attend my Weight Watchers meeting this week on _____

MARCH

1 9 8 9

MONDAY
13

TUESDAY
14

WEDNESDAY
15

THURSDAY
16

St. Patrick's Day

FRIDAY
17

SATURDAY
18

Palm Sunday

SUNDAY
19

	S	M	T	W	T	F	S
				1	2	3	4
F	5	6	7	8	9	10	11
E	12	13	14	15	16	17	18
B	19	20	21	22	23	24	25
	26	27	28				

	S	M	T	W	T	F	S
				1	2	3	4
M	5	6	7	8	9	10	11
A	12	13	14	15	16	17	18
R	19	20	21	22	23	24	25
	26	27	28	29	30	31	

	S	M	T	W	T	F	S
							1
A	2	3	4	5	6	7	8
P	9	10	11	12	13	14	15
R	16	17	18	19	20	21	22
	23	24	25	26	27	28	29
	30						

WEEKLY FOOD DIARY

	MONDAY	TUESDAY	WEDNESDAY	THURSDAY	FRIDAY	SATURDAY	SUNDAY
BREAKFAST							
LUNCH							
DINNER							
SNACKS							
DAILY TOTALS	FRUIT _____ VEG _____ FAT _____ PROTEIN _____ BREAD _____ MILK _____ FLOATING _____	FRUIT _____ VEG _____ FAT _____ PROTEIN _____ BREAD _____ MILK _____ FLOATING _____	FRUIT _____ VEG _____ FAT _____ PROTEIN _____ BREAD _____ MILK _____ FLOATING _____	FRUIT _____ VEG _____ FAT _____ PROTEIN _____ BREAD _____ MILK _____ FLOATING _____	FRUIT _____ VEG _____ FAT _____ PROTEIN _____ BREAD _____ MILK _____ FLOATING _____	FRUIT _____ VEG _____ FAT _____ PROTEIN _____ BREAD _____ MILK _____ FLOATING _____	FRUIT _____ VEG _____ FAT _____ PROTEIN _____ BREAD _____ MILK _____ FLOATING _____

WEEKLY LIMITS   EGGS _____   CHEESE _____   MEAT _____   ORGAN MEAT _____   OPTIONAL CALORIES _____

I will attend my Weight Watchers meeting this week on _____

MONDAY
20

TUESDAY
21

WEDNESDAY
22

THURSDAY
23

Good Friday

FRIDAY
24

SATURDAY
25

Easter Sunday

SUNDAY
26

	S	M	T	W	T	F	S
				1	2	3	4
F	5	6	7	8	9	10	11
E	12	13	14	15	16	17	18
B	19	20	21	22	23	24	25
	26	27	28				

	S	M	T	W	T	F	S
				1	2	3	4
M	5	6	7	8	9	10	11
A	12	13	14	15	16	17	18
R	19	20	21	22	23	24	25
	26	27	28	29	30	31	

	S	M	T	W	T	F	S
							1
A	2	3	4	5	6	7	8
P	9	10	11	12	13	14	15
R	16	17	18	19	20	21	22
	23	24	25	26	27	28	29
	30						

WEEKLY FOOD DIARY

	MONDAY	TUESDAY	WEDNESDAY	THURSDAY	FRIDAY	SATURDAY	SUNDAY
BREAKFAST							
LUNCH							
DINNER							
SNACKS							
DAILY TOTALS	FRUIT ___ VEG ___ FAT ___ PROTEIN ___ BREAD ___ MILK ___ FLOATING ___	FRUIT ___ VEG ___ FAT ___ PROTEIN ___ BREAD ___ MILK ___ FLOATING ___	FRUIT ___ VEG ___ FAT ___ PROTEIN ___ BREAD ___ MILK ___ FLOATING ___	FRUIT ___ VEG ___ FAT ___ PROTEIN ___ BREAD ___ MILK ___ FLOATING ___	FRUIT ___ VEG ___ FAT ___ PROTEIN ___ BREAD ___ MILK ___ FLOATING ___	FRUIT ___ VEG ___ FAT ___ PROTEIN ___ BREAD ___ MILK ___ FLOATING ___	FRUIT ___ VEG ___ FAT ___ PROTEIN ___ BREAD ___ MILK ___ FLOATING ___

WEEKLY LIMITS   EGGS _____   CHEESE _____   MEAT _____   ORGAN MEAT _____   OPTIONAL CALORIES _____

I will attend my Weight Watchers meeting this week on _____

Easter Monday (Canada)

MONDAY
27

TUESDAY
28

WEDNESDAY
29

THURSDAY
30

FRIDAY
31

SATURDAY
1

SUNDAY
2

	S	M	T	W	T	F	S
				1	2	3	4
F	5	6	7	8	9	10	11
E	12	13	14	15	16	17	18
B	19	20	21	22	23	24	25
	26	27	28				

	S	M	T	W	T	F	S
				1	2	3	4
M	5	6	7	8	9	10	11
A	12	13	14	15	16	17	18
R	19	20	21	22	23	24	25
	26	27	28	29	30	31	

	S	M	T	W	T	F	S
							1
A	2	3	4	5	6	7	8
P	9	10	11	12	13	14	15
R	16	17	18	19	20	21	22
	23	24	25	26	27	28	29
	30						

Baked Cheese-Topped Apple Slices

Makes 4 servings

An easy and elegant snack that makes a special dessert as well.

**½ pound Golden Delicious apples,
cored, pared, and cut crosswise into
thin slices**
1 tablespoon apple brandy
1 teaspoon lemon juice
½ teaspoon ground cinnamon

3 tablespoons whipped cream cheese
2 tablespoons granulated sugar
1 egg
1 teaspoon vanilla extract

Preheat oven to 375°F. In small mixing bowl combine apple slices, brandy, and lemon juice, tossing until combined. Spray 8- or 9-inch pie pan with nonstick cooking spray and arrange apple slices in pan, overlapping slightly; sprinkle with cinnamon.

Using electric mixer, in small mixing bowl combine remaining ingredients and beat at low speed until mixture is smooth and combined. Pour cream cheese mixture over apple slices and bake until golden brown, 15 to 20 minutes.

Each serving provides: ½ Fruit Exchange; 80 Optional Calories

Per serving: 111 calories; 2 g protein; 4 g fat; 15 g carbohydrate; 18 mg calcium; 39 mg sodium; 76 mg cholesterol; 1 g dietary fiber

Tomato 'n' Chives

Makes 2 servings

This wonderful combination of flavors will certainly start any meal off right.

**1 large tomato (about 7 ounces), cut
into ¼-inch-thick slices**
1 tablespoon chopped fresh chives

¼ cup orange juice (no sugar added)
**1 teaspoon *each* freshly squeezed lime
juice and olive oil**

Decoratively arrange tomato slices on serving platter; sprinkle with chives. Using a
wire whisk, in small mixing bowl combine remaining ingredients; pour over tomato
slices and chives and serve.

Each serving provides: 1½ Vegetable Exchanges; ½ Fat Exchange; 15 Optional Calories

Per serving: 54 calories; 1 g protein; 2 g fat; 8 g carbohydrate; 11 mg calcium; 8 mg sodium; 0 mg
cholesterol; 0.8 g dietary fiber

WEIGHT
RECIPE
WATCHERS

Shepherd's Pie

Makes 2 servings

A great way to use up leftover lamb.

2 teaspoons margarine
½ cup *each* **diced carrot and thoroughly washed leeks (white portion and some green)**
¼ cup diced celery
1 small garlic clove, minced
2 tablespoons all-purpose flour
1 packet instant beef broth and seasoning mix, dissolved in 1 cup hot water

¼ cup frozen peas
2 tablespoons chopped fresh mint
4 ounces boned cooked lamb, cut into ½-inch cubes
1 cup hot water
⅔ cup instant potato flakes

In 2-quart saucepan melt margarine; add carrot, leeks, celery, and garlic and sauté over medium heat, stirring occasionally, until leeks and celery are softened, 2 to 3 minutes. Sprinkle flour over vegetables and stir quickly to combine; cook, stirring constantly, for 1 minute. Gradually stir in dissolved broth mix; add peas and mint and stir to combine. Reduce heat to low and cook, stirring occasionally, until carrot is tender and mixture thickens, about 10 minutes. Add lamb and cook until heated through, 2 to 3 minutes.

Using a fork, in small mixing bowl combine water and potato flakes and mix until light and fluffy. Divide lamb mixture into two 1½-cup flameproof casseroles; top each with half of the potato mixture and spread over center of each casserole. Broil until potato mixture is lightly browned, 2 to 3 minutes.

Each serving provides: 2 Protein Exchanges; 1 Bread Exchange; 1¼ Vegetable Exchanges; 1 Fat Exchange; 55 Optional Calories

Per serving: 295 calories; 20 g protein; 8 g fat; 33 g carbohydrate; 108 mg calcium; 637 mg sodium; 57 mg cholesterol; 2 g dietary fiber

Vegetable Nachos

Makes 4 servings, 3 nachos each

½ cup diced tomato
¼ avocado (2 ounces), pared and diced
2 tablespoons sliced scallion (green onion)
1 tablespoon *each* seeded and chopped jalapeño pepper and chopped cilantro (Chinese parsley)*

2 flour tortillas (6-inch diameter each)
2 ounces Cheddar *or* Colby cheese, shredded
2 tablespoons sour cream
6 pitted black olives, each cut crosswise into 4 pieces

In small mixing bowl combine tomato, avocado, scallion, jalapeño pepper, and cilantro, mixing well; set aside. On nonstick baking sheet arrange tortillas in a single layer and broil 6 inches from heat source, turning once, until lightly browned, about 1 minute on each side. Spread half of the tomato mixture evenly over 1 side of each tortilla and broil until mixture is heated through, about 1 minute. Sprinkle each portion of tomato mixture with 1 ounce cheese and broil until cheese is melted and lightly browned, 1 to 2 minutes longer. Cut each tortilla into six equal wedges; top each wedge with ½ teaspoon sour cream and 2 olive pieces.

Each serving provides: ½ Protein Exchange, ½ Bread Exchange; ¼ Vegetable Exchange; 50 Optional Calories

Per serving with Cheddar: 144 calories; 5 g protein; 10 g fat; 9 g carbohydrate; 142 mg calcium; 206 mg sodium; 18 mg cholesterol; 0.8 g dietary fiber

With Colby: 143 calories; 5 g protein; 10 g fat; 9 g carbohydrate; 137 mg calcium; 203 mg sodium; 17 mg cholesterol; 1 g dietary fiber

* If cilantro is not available, Italian (flat-leaf) parsley may be substituted.

APRIL

SUNDAY	MONDAY	TUESDAY	WEDNESDAY
2	3	4	5
9	10	11	12
16	17	18	19
23 / 30	24	25	26

APRIL

THURSDAY	FRIDAY	SATURDAY	NOTES/GOALS
		1	
6	7	8	
13	14	15	
20	21	22	
27	28	29	

WEEKLY FOOD DIARY

	MONDAY	TUESDAY	WEDNESDAY	THURSDAY	FRIDAY	SATURDAY	SUNDAY
BREAKFAST							
LUNCH							
DINNER							
SNACKS							
DAILY TOTALS	FRUIT _____ VEG _____ FAT _____ PROTEIN _____ BREAD _____ MILK _____ FLOATING _____	FRUIT _____ VEG _____ FAT _____ PROTEIN _____ BREAD _____ MILK _____ FLOATING _____	FRUIT _____ VEG _____ FAT _____ PROTEIN _____ BREAD _____ MILK _____ FLOATING _____	FRUIT _____ VEG _____ FAT _____ PROTEIN _____ BREAD _____ MILK _____ FLOATING _____	FRUIT _____ VEG _____ FAT _____ PROTEIN _____ BREAD _____ MILK _____ FLOATING _____	FRUIT _____ VEG _____ FAT _____ PROTEIN _____ BREAD _____ MILK _____ FLOATING _____	FRUIT _____ VEG _____ FAT _____ PROTEIN _____ BREAD _____ MILK _____ FLOATING _____

WEEKLY LIMITS   EGGS _____   CHEESE _____   MEAT _____   ORGAN MEAT _____   OPTIONAL CALORIES _____

I will attend my Weight Watchers meeting this week on _____

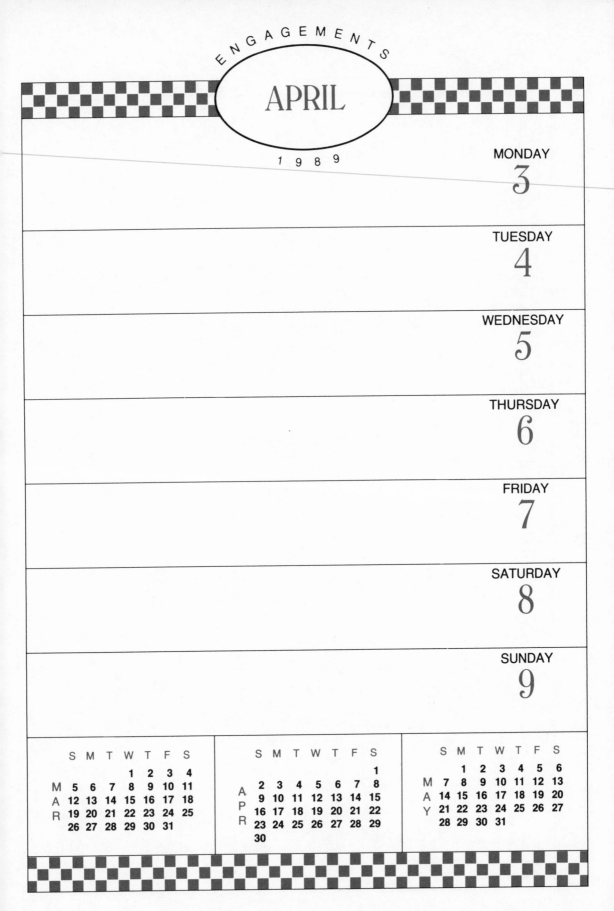

ENGAGEMENTS

APRIL

1 9 8 9

MONDAY
3

TUESDAY
4

WEDNESDAY
5

THURSDAY
6

FRIDAY
7

SATURDAY
8

SUNDAY
9

	S	M	T	W	T	F	S
				1	2	3	4
M	5	6	7	8	9	10	11
A	12	13	14	15	16	17	18
R	19	20	21	22	23	24	25
	26	27	28	29	30	31	

	S	M	T	W	T	F	S
							1
A	2	3	4	5	6	7	8
P	9	10	11	12	13	14	15
R	16	17	18	19	20	21	22
	23	24	25	26	27	28	29
	30						

	S	M	T	W	T	F	S
		1	2	3	4	5	6
M	7	8	9	10	11	12	13
A	14	15	16	17	18	19	20
Y	21	22	23	24	25	26	27
	28	29	30	31			

WEEKLY FOOD DIARY

	MONDAY	TUESDAY	WEDNESDAY	THURSDAY	FRIDAY	SATURDAY	SUNDAY
BREAKFAST							
LUNCH							
DINNER							
SNACKS							
DAILY TOTALS	FRUIT ___ VEG ___ FAT ___ PROTEIN ___ BREAD ___ MILK ___ FLOATING ___	FRUIT ___ VEG ___ FAT ___ PROTEIN ___ BREAD ___ MILK ___ FLOATING ___	FRUIT ___ VEG ___ FAT ___ PROTEIN ___ BREAD ___ MILK ___ FLOATING ___	FRUIT ___ VEG ___ FAT ___ PROTEIN ___ BREAD ___ MILK ___ FLOATING ___	FRUIT ___ VEG ___ FAT ___ PROTEIN ___ BREAD ___ MILK ___ FLOATING ___	FRUIT ___ VEG ___ FAT ___ PROTEIN ___ BREAD ___ MILK ___ FLOATING ___	FRUIT ___ VEG ___ FAT ___ PROTEIN ___ BREAD ___ MILK ___ FLOATING ___

WEEKLY LIMITS   EGGS ___   CHEESE ___   MEAT ___   ORGAN MEAT ___   OPTIONAL CALORIES ___

I will attend my Weight Watchers meeting this week on ___

APRIL

1989

MONDAY
10

TUESDAY
11

WEDNESDAY
12

THURSDAY
13

FRIDAY
14

SATURDAY
15

SUNDAY
16

	S	M	T	W	T	F	S
					1	2	3	4
M	5	6	7	8	9	10	11
A	12	13	14	15	16	17	18
R	19	20	21	22	23	24	25
	26	27	28	29	30	31	

	S	M	T	W	T	F	S
							1
A	2	3	4	5	6	7	8
P	9	10	11	12	13	14	15
R	16	17	18	19	20	21	22
	23	24	25	26	27	28	29
	30						

	S	M	T	W	T	F	S
		1	2	3	4	5	6
M	7	8	9	10	11	12	13
A	14	15	16	17	18	19	20
Y	21	22	23	24	25	26	27
	28	29	30	31			

WEEKLY FOOD DIARY

	MONDAY	TUESDAY	WEDNESDAY	THURSDAY	FRIDAY	SATURDAY	SUNDAY
BREAKFAST							
LUNCH							
DINNER							
SNACKS							
DAILY TOTALS	FRUIT ____ VEG ____ FAT ____ PROTEIN ____ BREAD ____ MILK ____ FLOATING ____	FRUIT ____ VEG ____ FAT ____ PROTEIN ____ BREAD ____ MILK ____ FLOATING ____	FRUIT ____ VEG ____ FAT ____ PROTEIN ____ BREAD ____ MILK ____ FLOATING ____	FRUIT ____ VEG ____ FAT ____ PROTEIN ____ BREAD ____ MILK ____ FLOATING ____	FRUIT ____ VEG ____ FAT ____ PROTEIN ____ BREAD ____ MILK ____ FLOATING ____	FRUIT ____ VEG ____ FAT ____ PROTEIN ____ BREAD ____ MILK ____ FLOATING ____	FRUIT ____ VEG ____ FAT ____ PROTEIN ____ BREAD ____ MILK ____ FLOATING ____

WEEKLY LIMITS EGGS _____ CHEESE _____ MEAT _____ ORGAN MEAT _____ OPTIONAL CALORIES _____

I will attend my Weight Watchers meeting this week on _____

APRIL

1 9 8 9

MONDAY
17

TUESDAY
18

WEDNESDAY
19

First Day of Passover

THURSDAY
20

FRIDAY
21

SATURDAY
22

SUNDAY
23

	S	M	T	W	T	F	S
					1	2	3	4
M	5	6	7	8	9	10	11
A	12	13	14	15	16	17	18
R	19	20	21	22	23	24	25
	26	27	28	29	30	31	

	S	M	T	W	T	F	S
							1
A	2	3	4	5	6	7	8
P	9	10	11	12	13	14	15
R	16	17	18	19	20	21	22
	23	24	25	26	27	28	29
	30						

	S	M	T	W	T	F	S
	1	2	3	4	5	6
M	7	8	9	10	11	12	13
A	14	15	16	17	18	19	20
Y	21	22	23	24	25	26	27
	28	29	30	31			

WEEKLY FOOD DIARY

	MONDAY	TUESDAY	WEDNESDAY	THURSDAY	FRIDAY	SATURDAY	SUNDAY
BREAKFAST							
LUNCH							
DINNER							
SNACKS							
DAILY TOTALS	FRUIT ___ VEG ___ FAT ___ PROTEIN ___ BREAD ___ MILK ___ FLOATING ___	FRUIT ___ VEG ___ FAT ___ PROTEIN ___ BREAD ___ MILK ___ FLOATING ___	FRUIT ___ VEG ___ FAT ___ PROTEIN ___ BREAD ___ MILK ___ FLOATING ___	FRUIT ___ VEG ___ FAT ___ PROTEIN ___ BREAD ___ MILK ___ FLOATING ___	FRUIT ___ VEG ___ FAT ___ PROTEIN ___ BREAD ___ MILK ___ FLOATING ___	FRUIT ___ VEG ___ FAT ___ PROTEIN ___ BREAD ___ MILK ___ FLOATING ___	FRUIT ___ VEG ___ FAT ___ PROTEIN ___ BREAD ___ MILK ___ FLOATING ___

WEEKLY LIMITS   EGGS _____   CHEESE _____   MEAT _____   ORGAN MEAT _____   OPTIONAL CALORIES _____

I will attend my Weight Watchers meeting this week on _____

ENGAGEMENTS

APRIL

1989

	MONDAY 24
	TUESDAY 25
	WEDNESDAY 26
	THURSDAY 27
	FRIDAY 28
	SATURDAY 29
	SUNDAY 30

	S	M	T	W	T	F	S
					1	2	3	4
M	5	6	7	8	9	10	11
A	12	13	14	15	16	17	18
R	19	20	21	22	23	24	25
	26	27	28	29	30	31	

	S	M	T	W	T	F	S
							1
A	2	3	4	5	6	7	8
P	9	10	11	12	13	14	15
R	16	17	18	19	20	21	22
	23	24	25	26	27	28	29
	30						

	S	M	T	W	T	F	S
		1	2	3	4	5	6
M	7	8	9	10	11	12	13
A	14	15	16	17	18	19	20
Y	21	22	23	24	25	26	27
	28	29	30	31			

WEIGHT
RECIPE
WATCHERS

Fluffy Apple Omelet

Makes 2 servings

1 tablespoon sweet butter, divided
1 small Granny Smith apple (about
   ¼ pound), cored, pared, and diced
2 tablespoons finely diced onion
3 eggs (at room temperature)
Salt

1 tablespoon water
Dash pepper
1 ounce Monterey Jack cheese,
   shredded, divided
1 teaspoon granulated sugar
¼ teaspoon ground cinnamon

In 8-inch nonstick skillet that has a metal or removable handle melt 1½ teaspoons butter; add apple and onion and sauté over medium-high heat until onion is translucent, about 2 minutes. Remove from heat and let cool.

Preheat oven to 425°F. Separate 2 eggs. Using electric mixer, in medium mixing bowl beat egg whites and dash salt at high speed until soft peaks form; set aside. Using a wire whisk, in large mixing bowl combine remaining egg, the egg yolks, ¼ teaspoon salt, the water, and pepper and beat until combined. Stir half the beaten egg whites into yolk mixture, then fold in remaining whites, apple mixture, and ½ ounce cheese.

Wipe out skillet with paper towels; add remaining 1½ teaspoons butter and melt over medium heat. Carefully pour omelet mixture into pan, then sprinkle with remaining ½ ounce cheese. Cook over medium heat until bottom of omelet is firm and lightly browned, 4 to 5 minutes. Transfer skillet to oven and bake until top of omelet is golden brown and a knife, inserted in center, comes out clean, about 10 minutes. Sprinkle sugar and cinnamon over omelet; using a spatula, loosen edges of omelet and slide onto serving platter. To serve, cut omelet in half.

Each serving provides: 2 Protein Exchanges; ⅛ Vegetable Exchange; ½ Fruit Exchange; 60 Optional Calories

Per serving: 262 calories; 13 g protein; 19 g fat; 11 g carbohydrate; 160 mg calcium; 517 mg sodium; 439 mg cholesterol; 1 g dietary fiber

Greek-Style Lamburgers

Makes 2 servings, 1 patty each

4 ounces ground lamb
1 ounce feta cheese, crumbled

1½ teaspoons chopped fresh mint *or*
½ teaspoon dried
⅛ teaspoon *each* salt and pepper

In medium mixing bowl thoroughly combine all ingredients; shape mixture into 2 equal patties. Spray rack in broiling pan with nonstick cooking spray; arrange patties on rack and broil, turning once, 4 to 5 minutes on each side or until done to taste.

Each serving provides: 2 Protein Exchanges

Per serving: 125 calories; 13 g protein; 7 g fat; 1 g carbohydrate; 77 mg calcium; 325 mg sodium; 55 mg cholesterol; 0 g dietary fiber

WEIGHT RECIPE WATCHERS

"Peach Melba" Smoothie

Makes 2 servings, about ¾ cup each

This filling, frothy beverage hits the spot at snack time.

½ cup canned peach slices (no sugar added)
½ cup low-fat milk (1% milk fat)
¼ cup plain low-fat yogurt

1 teaspoon *each* granulated sugar and raspberry syrup
3 to 4 ice cubes

Chill two 8-ounce glasses. In blender container combine all ingredients except ice cubes and process until smooth. With motor running add ice cubes, 1 at a time, processing after each addition, until ice is dissolved (mixture should be smooth and frothy). Pour half of mixture into each chilled glass and serve immediately.

Each serving provides: ½ Fruit Exchange; ½ Milk Exchange; 25 Optional Calories

Per serving: 74 calories; 4 g protein; 1 g fat; 13 g carbohydrate; 128 mg calcium; 52 mg sodium; 4 mg cholesterol; 1 g dietary fiber

WEIGHT
RECIPE
WATCHERS

Asparagus Deviled Eggs

Makes 4 servings, 2 halves each

A special springtime appetizer or light lunch.

4 eggs, hard-cooked and chilled
½ cup cooked sliced asparagus
(reserve 8 pieces for garnish)

1 tablespoon Dijon-style mustard
Dash white pepper

Cut eggs lengthwise into halves. Carefully remove yolks from egg halves to work bowl of food processor fitted with steel blade; set whites aside. Add asparagus to yolks and process, using on-off motion, until combined (*do not puree*). Stir in mustard and pepper.

Using a spoon, fill each reserved white half with ⅛ of the yolk mixture (about 1 tablespoon plus 1½ teaspoons). Garnish each egg half with reserved asparagus piece. Arrange eggs on serving platter and serve immediately or cover loosely and refrigerate until ready to serve.

Each serving provides: 1 Protein Exchange; ¼ Vegetable Exchange

Per serving: 89 calories; 7 g protein; 6 g fat; 2 g carbohydrate; 33 mg calcium; 181 mg sodium; 274 mg cholesterol; 0.8 g dietary fiber

MAY

SUNDAY	MONDAY	TUESDAY	WEDNESDAY
	1	2	3
7	8	9	10
14	15	16	17
21	22	23	24
28	29	30	31

THURSDAY	FRIDAY	SATURDAY	NOTES/GOALS
4	5	6	
11	12	13	
18	19	20	
25	26	27	

WEEKLY FOOD DIARY

	MONDAY	TUESDAY	WEDNESDAY	THURSDAY	FRIDAY	SATURDAY	SUNDAY
BREAKFAST							
LUNCH							
DINNER							
SNACKS							
DAILY TOTALS	FRUIT ___ VEG ___ FAT ___ PROTEIN ___ BREAD ___ MILK ___ FLOATING ___	FRUIT ___ VEG ___ FAT ___ PROTEIN ___ BREAD ___ MILK ___ FLOATING ___	FRUIT ___ VEG ___ FAT ___ PROTEIN ___ BREAD ___ MILK ___ FLOATING ___	FRUIT ___ VEG ___ FAT ___ PROTEIN ___ BREAD ___ MILK ___ FLOATING ___	FRUIT ___ VEG ___ FAT ___ PROTEIN ___ BREAD ___ MILK ___ FLOATING ___	FRUIT ___ VEG ___ FAT ___ PROTEIN ___ BREAD ___ MILK ___ FLOATING ___	FRUIT ___ VEG ___ FAT ___ PROTEIN ___ BREAD ___ MILK ___ FLOATING ___

WEEKLY LIMITS EGGS _____ CHEESE _____ MEAT _____ ORGAN MEAT _____ OPTIONAL CALORIES _____

I will attend my Weight Watchers meeting this week on _____

MAY

1 9 8 9

MONDAY
1

TUESDAY
2

WEDNESDAY
3

THURSDAY
4

FRIDAY
5

SATURDAY
6

SUNDAY
7

	S	M	T	W	T	F	S
							1
APR	2	3	4	5	6	7	8
	9	10	11	12	13	14	15
	16	17	18	19	20	21	22
	23	24	25	26	27	28	29
	30						

	S	M	T	W	T	F	S
		1	2	3	4	5	6
M	7	8	9	10	11	12	13
A	14	15	16	17	18	19	20
Y	21	22	23	24	25	26	27
	28	29	30	31			

	S	M	T	W	T	F	S
					1	2	3
JUNE	4	5	6	7	8	9	10
	11	12	13	14	15	16	17
	18	19	20	21	22	23	24
	25	26	27	28	29	30	

WEEKLY FOOD DIARY

	MONDAY	TUESDAY	WEDNESDAY	THURSDAY	FRIDAY	SATURDAY	SUNDAY
BREAKFAST							
LUNCH							
DINNER							
SNACKS							
DAILY TOTALS	FRUIT ___ VEG ___ FAT ___ PROTEIN ___ BREAD ___ MILK ___ FLOATING ___	FRUIT ___ VEG ___ FAT ___ PROTEIN ___ BREAD ___ MILK ___ FLOATING ___	FRUIT ___ VEG ___ FAT ___ PROTEIN ___ BREAD ___ MILK ___ FLOATING ___	FRUIT ___ VEG ___ FAT ___ PROTEIN ___ BREAD ___ MILK ___ FLOATING ___	FRUIT ___ VEG ___ FAT ___ PROTEIN ___ BREAD ___ MILK ___ FLOATING ___	FRUIT ___ VEG ___ FAT ___ PROTEIN ___ BREAD ___ MILK ___ FLOATING ___	FRUIT ___ VEG ___ FAT ___ PROTEIN ___ BREAD ___ MILK ___ FLOATING ___

WEEKLY LIMITS EGGS _____ CHEESE _____ MEAT _____ ORGAN MEAT _____ OPTIONAL CALORIES _____

I will attend my Weight Watchers meeting this week on _____

ENGAGEMENTS

MAY

1989

MONDAY
8

TUESDAY
9

WEDNESDAY
10

THURSDAY
11

FRIDAY
12

SATURDAY
13

Mother's Day

SUNDAY
14

	S	M	T	W	T	F	S
							1
A	2	3	4	5	6	7	8
P	9	10	11	12	13	14	15
R	16	17	18	19	20	21	22
	23	24	25	26	27	28	29
	30						

	S	M	T	W	T	F	S
		1	2	3	4	5	6
M	7	8	9	10	11	12	13
A	14	15	16	17	18	19	20
Y	21	22	23	24	25	26	27
	28	29	30	31			

	S	M	T	W	T	F	S
					1	2	3
J	4	5	6	7	8	9	10
U	11	12	13	14	15	16	17
N	18	19	20	21	22	23	24
E	25	26	27	28	29	30	

WEEKLY FOOD DIARY

	MONDAY	TUESDAY	WEDNESDAY	THURSDAY	FRIDAY	SATURDAY	SUNDAY
BREAKFAST							
LUNCH							
DINNER							
SNACKS							
DAILY TOTALS	FRUIT ___ VEG ___ FAT ___ PROTEIN ___ BREAD ___ MILK ___ FLOATING ___	FRUIT ___ VEG ___ FAT ___ PROTEIN ___ BREAD ___ MILK ___ FLOATING ___	FRUIT ___ VEG ___ FAT ___ PROTEIN ___ BREAD ___ MILK ___ FLOATING ___	FRUIT ___ VEG ___ FAT ___ PROTEIN ___ BREAD ___ MILK ___ FLOATING ___	FRUIT ___ VEG ___ FAT ___ PROTEIN ___ BREAD ___ MILK ___ FLOATING ___	FRUIT ___ VEG ___ FAT ___ PROTEIN ___ BREAD ___ MILK ___ FLOATING ___	FRUIT ___ VEG ___ FAT ___ PROTEIN ___ BREAD ___ MILK ___ FLOATING ___

WEEKLY LIMITS EGGS _____ CHEESE _____ MEAT _____ ORGAN MEAT _____ OPTIONAL CALORIES _____

I will attend my Weight Watchers meeting this week on _____

Weight Watchers 26th Anniversary

MONDAY
15

TUESDAY
16

WEDNESDAY
17

THURSDAY
18

FRIDAY
19

Armed Forces Day

SATURDAY
20

SUNDAY
21

	S	M	T	W	T	F	S
							1
A	2	3	4	5	6	7	8
P	9	10	11	12	13	14	15
R	16	17	18	19	20	21	22
	23	24	25	26	27	28	29
	30						

	S	M	T	W	T	F	S
		1	2	3	4	5	6
M	7	8	9	10	11	12	13
A	14	15	16	17	18	19	20
Y	21	22	23	24	25	26	27
	28	29	30	31			

	S	M	T	W	T	F	S
J					1	2	3
U	4	5	6	7	8	9	10
N	11	12	13	14	15	16	17
E	18	19	20	21	22	23	24
	25	26	27	28	29	30	

WEEKLY FOOD DIARY

	MONDAY	TUESDAY	WEDNESDAY	THURSDAY	FRIDAY	SATURDAY	SUNDAY
BREAKFAST							
LUNCH							
DINNER							
SNACKS							
DAILY TOTALS	FRUIT ___ VEG ___ FAT ___ PROTEIN ___ BREAD ___ MILK ___ FLOATING ___	FRUIT ___ VEG ___ FAT ___ PROTEIN ___ BREAD ___ MILK ___ FLOATING ___	FRUIT ___ VEG ___ FAT ___ PROTEIN ___ BREAD ___ MILK ___ FLOATING ___	FRUIT ___ VEG ___ FAT ___ PROTEIN ___ BREAD ___ MILK ___ FLOATING ___	FRUIT ___ VEG ___ FAT ___ PROTEIN ___ BREAD ___ MILK ___ FLOATING ___	FRUIT ___ VEG ___ FAT ___ PROTEIN ___ BREAD ___ MILK ___ FLOATING ___	FRUIT ___ VEG ___ FAT ___ PROTEIN ___ BREAD ___ MILK ___ FLOATING ___

WEEKLY LIMITS EGGS _____ CHEESE _____ MEAT _____ ORGAN MEAT _____ OPTIONAL CALORIES _____

I will attend my Weight Watchers meeting this week on _____

MAY

1 9 8 9

Victoria Day (Canada)

MONDAY
22

TUESDAY
23

WEDNESDAY
24

THURSDAY
25

FRIDAY
26

SATURDAY
27

SUNDAY
28

	S	M	T	W	T	F	S
							1
A	2	3	4	5	6	7	8
P	9	10	11	12	13	14	15
R	16	17	18	19	20	21	22
	23	24	25	26	27	28	29
	30						

	S	M	T	W	T	F	S
		1	2	3	4	5	6
M	7	8	9	10	11	12	13
A	14	15	16	17	18	19	20
Y	21	22	23	24	25	26	27
	28	29	30	31			

	S	M	T	W	T	F	S
					1	2	3
J	4	5	6	7	8	9	10
U	11	12	13	14	15	16	17
N	18	19	20	21	22	23	24
E	25	26	27	28	29	30	

WEIGHT
RECIPE
WATCHERS

Fresh Vegetables with Mustard Dipping Sauce

Makes 2 servings

If available, country Dijon-style mustard, which is grainy in texture, is excellent in this flavorful dipping sauce.

¼ cup plain low-fat yogurt
1 tablespoon plus 1½ teaspoons sour cream
1 tablespoon Dijon-style mustard

1½ teaspoons *each* cider vinegar and honey
½ cup *each* sliced mushrooms, green, red, *or* yellow bell pepper strips, diagonally sliced carrot, and broccoli florets

Using a wire whisk, in small mixing bowl combine yogurt, sour cream, mustard, vinegar, and honey. Cover with plastic wrap and refrigerate until ready to serve.

To serve, decoratively arrange vegetables on serving platter and serve with mustard sauce.

Each serving provides: 2 Vegetable Exchanges; ¼ Milk Exchange; 40 Optional Calories

Per serving: 87 calories; 4 g protein; 2 g fat; 15 g carbohydrate; 82 mg calcium; 266 mg sodium; 3 mg cholesterol; 1 g dietary fiber

Sweet Pepper Spread

Makes 2 servings, 6 leaves each

Use this colorful and delicious spread as a filling for mushroom caps, a spread on cucumber slices, or to stuff celery ribs or endive leaves. It makes an elegant appetizer.

1 medium red *or* green bell pepper
3 tablespoons whipped cream cheese

1 tablespoon finely minced onion, *or*
scallion (green onion), *or* shallot

Preheat broiler. On baking sheet lined with heavy-duty foil broil bell pepper 3 inches from heat source, turning frequently, until charred on all sides; let stand until cool enough to handle, 15 to 20 minutes.

Peel pepper; remove and discard stem ends and seeds. Cut pepper into pieces and transfer to small mixing bowl. Using a fork, mash pepper; add cheese and onion (or scallion or shallot) and stir until combined. Use immediately or cover and refrigerate for up to 1 day.

Each serving provides: 1 Vegetable Exchange, 50 Optional Calories

Per serving with scallion: 61 calories; 1 g protein; 5 g fat; 3 g carbohydrate; 17 mg calcium; 43 mg sodium; 16 mg cholesterol; 0.5 g dietary fiber

With shallot: 64 calories; 2 g protein; 5 g fat; 4 g carbohydrate; 17 mg calcium; 44 mg sodium; 16 mg cholesterol; 0.5 g dietary fiber

WEIGHT

RECIPE

WATCHERS

Warm Chicken Salad with Papaya

Makes 2 servings

5 ounces skinned and boned chicken breast
2 tablespoons *each* **freshly squeezed lime juice, divided, and soy sauce**
2 teaspoons olive oil
½ ounce shelled pecans
½ cup orange juice (no sugar added)

1 tablespoon *each* **chopped fresh mint and raspberry vinegar, seasoned rice vinegar,** *or* **cider vinegar**
8 lettuce leaves
½ medium papaya (about 8 ounces), pared, seeded, and thinly sliced

Set chicken in shallow glass or stainless-steel bowl (not aluminum*). In small bowl combine 1 tablespoon lime juice and the soy sauce; pour over chicken. Cover with plastic wrap and refrigerate overnight or at least 30 minutes.

In 8-inch nonstick skillet heat oil; add pecans and sauté over medium heat, stirring frequently, until nuts are toasted, about 1 minute. Using slotted spoon, remove pecans from skillet and set aside. To skillet containing oil add remaining tablespoon lime juice, the orange juice, mint, and vinegar and stir to combine; set aside.

Transfer chicken to broiling pan, discarding marinade, and broil, turning once, until chicken is cooked through, 3 to 4 minutes on each side.

To serve, arrange lettuce leaves on serving platter. Diagonally slice chicken. Decoratively arrange chicken and papaya slices on lettuce leaves; sprinkle with pecans. Stir orange juice mixture and pour over salad.

Each serving provides: 2 Protein Exchanges; 1 Vegetable Exchange; 1 Fat Exchange; 1 Fruit Exchange; 55 Optional Calories.

Per serving: 256 calories; 22 g protein; 11 g fat; 19 g carbohydrate; 70 mg calcium; 577 mg sodium; 49 mg cholesterol; 2 g dietary fiber

* It's best to marinate in glass or stainless-steel containers; acidic ingredients such as lime juice may react with aluminum, causing color and flavor changes.

Strawberry-Yogurt Gel

Makes 4 servings

¾ cup boiling water
1 envelope (four ½-cup servings) low-
   calorie strawberry-flavored gelatin
   (8 calories per ½ cup)
6 to 8 ice cubes

½ cup cold water
1 cup *each* plain low-fat yogurt and
   strawberries
½ cup thawed frozen dairy whipped
   topping

In medium heatproof bowl combine boiling water and gelatin and stir until gelatin is completely dissolved. Stir in ice cubes and cold water, stirring until ice is dissolved. Add yogurt and mix well until thoroughly combined.

Set aside 4 whole strawberries. Cut remaining strawberries into quarters and arrange ¼ of the berries in each of 4 dessert dishes. Top each portion with ¼ of the gelatin mixture; cover with plastic wrap and refrigerate until gelatin is set, about 1 hour. To serve, top each portion with 2 tablespoons whipped topping and 1 reserved strawberry.

Each serving provides: ½ Milk Exchange; 50 Optional Calories

Per serving: 79 calories; 4 g protein; 3 g fat; 9 g carbohydrate; 109 mg calcium; 110 mg sodium; 3 mg cholesterol; 0.7 g dietary fiber

JUNE

SUNDAY	MONDAY	TUESDAY	WEDNESDAY
4	5	6	7
11	12	13	14
18	19	20	21
25	26	27	28

JUNE

THURSDAY	FRIDAY	SATURDAY	NOTES/GOALS
1	2	3	
8	9	10	
15	16	17	
22	23	24	
29	30		

WEEKLY FOOD DIARY

	MONDAY	TUESDAY	WEDNESDAY	THURSDAY	FRIDAY	SATURDAY	SUNDAY
BREAKFAST							
LUNCH							
DINNER							
SNACKS							
DAILY TOTALS	FRUIT ___ VEG ___ FAT ___ PROTEIN ___ BREAD ___ MILK ___ FLOATING ___	FRUIT ___ VEG ___ FAT ___ PROTEIN ___ BREAD ___ MILK ___ FLOATING ___	FRUIT ___ VEG ___ FAT ___ PROTEIN ___ BREAD ___ MILK ___ FLOATING ___	FRUIT ___ VEG ___ FAT ___ PROTEIN ___ BREAD ___ MILK ___ FLOATING ___	FRUIT ___ VEG ___ FAT ___ PROTEIN ___ BREAD ___ MILK ___ FLOATING ___	FRUIT ___ VEG ___ FAT ___ PROTEIN ___ BREAD ___ MILK ___ FLOATING ___	FRUIT ___ VEG ___ FAT ___ PROTEIN ___ BREAD ___ MILK ___ FLOATING ___

WEEKLY LIMITS   EGGS _____   CHEESE _____   MEAT _____   ORGAN MEAT _____   OPTIONAL CALORIES _____

I will attend my Weight Watchers meeting this week on _____

MAY
JUNE

Memorial Day (observed)

MONDAY
29

Memorial Day

TUESDAY
30

WEDNESDAY
31

THURSDAY
1

FRIDAY
2

SATURDAY
3

SUNDAY
4

	S	M	T	W	T	F	S
		1	2	3	4	5	6
M	7	8	9	10	11	12	13
A	14	15	16	17	18	19	20
Y	21	22	23	24	25	26	27
	28	29	30	31			

	S	M	T	W	T	F	S
					1	2	3
J	4	5	6	7	8	9	10
U	11	12	13	14	15	16	17
N	18	19	20	21	22	23	24
E	25	26	27	28	29	30	

	S	M	T	W	T	F	S
							1
J	2	3	4	5	6	7	8
U	9	10	11	12	13	14	15
L	16	17	18	19	20	21	22
Y	23	24	25	26	27	28	29
	30	31					

WEEKLY FOOD DIARY

	MONDAY	TUESDAY	WEDNESDAY	THURSDAY	FRIDAY	SATURDAY	SUNDAY
BREAKFAST							
LUNCH							
DINNER							
SNACKS							
DAILY TOTALS	FRUIT ___ VEG ___ FAT ___ PROTEIN ___ BREAD ___ MILK ___ FLOATING ___	FRUIT ___ VEG ___ FAT ___ PROTEIN ___ BREAD ___ MILK ___ FLOATING ___	FRUIT ___ VEG ___ FAT ___ PROTEIN ___ BREAD ___ MILK ___ FLOATING ___	FRUIT ___ VEG ___ FAT ___ PROTEIN ___ BREAD ___ MILK ___ FLOATING ___	FRUIT ___ VEG ___ FAT ___ PROTEIN ___ BREAD ___ MILK ___ FLOATING ___	FRUIT ___ VEG ___ FAT ___ PROTEIN ___ BREAD ___ MILK ___ FLOATING ___	FRUIT ___ VEG ___ FAT ___ PROTEIN ___ BREAD ___ MILK ___ FLOATING ___

WEEKLY LIMITS   EGGS _____   CHEESE _____   MEAT _____   ORGAN MEAT _____   OPTIONAL CALORIES _____

I will attend my Weight Watchers meeting this week on _____

JUNE

1989

MONDAY
5

TUESDAY
6

WEDNESDAY
7

THURSDAY
8

FRIDAY
9

SATURDAY
10

SUNDAY
11

	S	M	T	W	T	F	S
		1	2	3	4	5	6
M	7	8	9	10	11	12	13
A	14	15	16	17	18	19	20
Y	21	22	23	24	25	26	27
	28	29	30	31			

	S	M	T	W	T	F	S
J					1	2	3
U	4	5	6	7	8	9	10
N	11	12	13	14	15	16	17
E	18	19	20	21	22	23	24
	25	26	27	28	29	30	

	S	M	T	W	T	F	S
J							1
U	2	3	4	5	6	7	8
L	9	10	11	12	13	14	15
Y	16	17	18	19	20	21	22
	23	24	25	26	27	28	29
	30	31					

WEEKLY FOOD DIARY

	MONDAY	TUESDAY	WEDNESDAY	THURSDAY	FRIDAY	SATURDAY	SUNDAY
BREAKFAST							
LUNCH							
DINNER							
SNACKS							
DAILY TOTALS	FRUIT ___ VEG ___ FAT ___ PROTEIN ___ BREAD ___ MILK ___ FLOATING ___	FRUIT ___ VEG ___ FAT ___ PROTEIN ___ BREAD ___ MILK ___ FLOATING ___	FRUIT ___ VEG ___ FAT ___ PROTEIN ___ BREAD ___ MILK ___ FLOATING ___	FRUIT ___ VEG ___ FAT ___ PROTEIN ___ BREAD ___ MILK ___ FLOATING ___	FRUIT ___ VEG ___ FAT ___ PROTEIN ___ BREAD ___ MILK ___ FLOATING ___	FRUIT ___ VEG ___ FAT ___ PROTEIN ___ BREAD ___ MILK ___ FLOATING ___	FRUIT ___ VEG ___ FAT ___ PROTEIN ___ BREAD ___ MILK ___ FLOATING ___

WEEKLY LIMITS   EGGS _____   CHEESE _____   MEAT _____   ORGAN MEAT _____   OPTIONAL CALORIES _____

I will attend my Weight Watchers meeting this week on _____

JUNE

1 9 8 9

MONDAY
12

TUESDAY
13

Flag Day

WEDNESDAY
14

THURSDAY
15

FRIDAY
16

SATURDAY
17

Father's Day

SUNDAY
18

	S	M	T	W	T	F	S
		1	2	3	4	5	6
M	7	8	9	10	11	12	13
A	14	15	16	17	18	19	20
Y	21	22	23	24	25	26	27
	28	29	30	31			

	S	M	T	W	T	F	S
J					1	2	3
U	4	5	6	7	8	9	10
N	11	12	13	14	15	16	17
E	18	19	20	21	22	23	24
	25	26	27	28	29	30	

	S	M	T	W	T	F	S
J							1
U	2	3	4	5	6	7	8
L	9	10	11	12	13	14	15
Y	16	17	18	19	20	21	22
	23	24	25	26	27	28	29
	30	31					

WEEKLY FOOD DIARY

	MONDAY	TUESDAY	WEDNESDAY	THURSDAY	FRIDAY	SATURDAY	SUNDAY
BREAKFAST							
LUNCH							
DINNER							
SNACKS							
DAILY TOTALS	FRUIT ___ VEG ___ FAT ___ PROTEIN ___ BREAD ___ MILK ___ FLOATING ___	FRUIT ___ VEG ___ FAT ___ PROTEIN ___ BREAD ___ MILK ___ FLOATING ___	FRUIT ___ VEG ___ FAT ___ PROTEIN ___ BREAD ___ MILK ___ FLOATING ___	FRUIT ___ VEG ___ FAT ___ PROTEIN ___ BREAD ___ MILK ___ FLOATING ___	FRUIT ___ VEG ___ FAT ___ PROTEIN ___ BREAD ___ MILK ___ FLOATING ___	FRUIT ___ VEG ___ FAT ___ PROTEIN ___ BREAD ___ MILK ___ FLOATING ___	FRUIT ___ VEG ___ FAT ___ PROTEIN ___ BREAD ___ MILK ___ FLOATING ___

WEEKLY LIMITS EGGS _____ CHEESE _____ MEAT _____ ORGAN MEAT _____ OPTIONAL CALORIES _____

I will attend my Weight Watchers meeting this week on _____

JUNE

1 9 8 9

MONDAY
19

TUESDAY
20

WEDNESDAY
21

THURSDAY
22

FRIDAY
23

SATURDAY
24

SUNDAY
25

	S	M	T	W	T	F	S
		1	2	3	4	5	6
M	7	8	9	10	11	12	13
A	14	15	16	17	18	19	20
Y	21	22	23	24	25	26	27
	28	29	30	31			

	S	M	T	W	T	F	S
J					1	2	3
U	4	5	6	7	8	9	10
N	11	12	13	14	15	16	17
E	18	19	20	21	22	23	24
	25	26	27	28	29	30	

	S	M	T	W	T	F	S
J							1
U	2	3	4	5	6	7	8
L	9	10	11	12	13	14	15
Y	16	17	18	19	20	21	22
	23	24	25	26	27	28	29
	30	31					

WEEKLY FOOD DIARY

	MONDAY	TUESDAY	WEDNESDAY	THURSDAY	FRIDAY	SATURDAY	SUNDAY
BREAKFAST							
LUNCH							
DINNER							
SNACKS							
DAILY TOTALS	FRUIT ___ VEG ___ FAT ___ PROTEIN ___ BREAD ___ MILK ___ FLOATING ___	FRUIT ___ VEG ___ FAT ___ PROTEIN ___ BREAD ___ MILK ___ FLOATING ___	FRUIT ___ VEG ___ FAT ___ PROTEIN ___ BREAD ___ MILK ___ FLOATING ___	FRUIT ___ VEG ___ FAT ___ PROTEIN ___ BREAD ___ MILK ___ FLOATING ___	FRUIT ___ VEG ___ FAT ___ PROTEIN ___ BREAD ___ MILK ___ FLOATING ___	FRUIT ___ VEG ___ FAT ___ PROTEIN ___ BREAD ___ MILK ___ FLOATING ___	FRUIT ___ VEG ___ FAT ___ PROTEIN ___ BREAD ___ MILK ___ FLOATING ___

WEEKLY LIMITS EGGS _____ CHEESE _____ MEAT _____ ORGAN MEAT _____ OPTIONAL CALORIES _____

I will attend my Weight Watchers meeting this week on _____

ENGAGEMENTS

JUNE
JULY

1989

MONDAY
26

TUESDAY
27

WEDNESDAY
28

THURSDAY
29

FRIDAY
30

Canada Day (Canada)

SATURDAY
1

SUNDAY
2

	S	M	T	W	T	F	S
		1	2	3	4	5	6
M	7	8	9	10	11	12	13
A	14	15	16	17	18	19	20
Y	21	22	23	24	25	26	27
	28	29	30	31			

	S	M	T	W	T	F	S
J					1	2	3
U	4	5	6	7	8	9	10
N	11	12	13	14	15	16	17
E	18	19	20	21	22	23	24
	25	26	27	28	29	30	

	S	M	T	W	T	F	S
J							1
U	2	3	4	5	6	7	8
L	9	10	11	12	13	14	15
Y	16	17	18	19	20	21	22
	23	24	25	26	27	28	29
	30	31					

Warm Salad of Salmon with Wild Mushrooms

Makes 2 servings

If shiitakes are unavailable, regular mushrooms are a suitable alternative.

2 teaspoons olive oil
2 cups shiitake mushrooms, sliced
1 medium yellow, red, *or* green bell pepper, seeded and cut into long thin strips
¼ cup thoroughly washed sliced leek (white portion and some green)
1 garlic clove, minced
½ cup canned ready-to-serve chicken broth

2 tablespoons raspberry vinegar, seasoned rice vinegar, *or* lemon juice
5-ounce salmon fillet, cut in half
6 lettuce leaves
1 tablespoon sour cream

In 10-inch nonstick skillet heat oil; add mushrooms, bell pepper, leek, and garlic and sauté over medium-high heat until vegetables are softened, 1 to 2 minutes.

In 1-cup liquid measure combine broth and vinegar (or lemon juice); arrange salmon over vegetables in skillet and top evenly with broth mixture. Reduce heat to medium-low; cover and cook until fish flakes easily when tested with a fork, 4 to 5 minutes (timing will depend on thickness of fillet).

On serving platter arrange lettuce leaves. Using a slotted spoon, remove salmon and vegetable mixture from skillet and arrange on lettuce; set aside. Set skillet with pan juices over high heat; stir in sour cream and cook, stirring occasionally, until mixture is creamy and thickens slightly, 1 to 2 minutes (*do not boil*). Pour sour cream mixture over salmon and vegetables and serve immediately.

Each serving provides: 2 Protein Exchanges; 4 Vegetable Exchanges; 1 Fat Exchange; 25 Optional Calories

Per serving: 196 calories; 18 g protein; 10 g fat; 11 g carbohydrate; 69 mg calcium; 315 mg sodium; 40 mg cholesterol; 4 g dietary fiber

Jicama and Orange Salad

Makes 2 servings

What looks like a turnip and tastes like a water chestnut? Why it's jicama, of course, starring in our tasty salad.

- 1 small orange (about 6 ounces), peeled
- 2 cups torn lettuce
- ½ cup julienne-cut pared jicama
- 1 tablespoon sliced scallion (green onion), green portion only
- 1½ teaspoons minced fresh mint *or* basil
- 1 teaspoon sunflower seed
- 2 teaspoons olive oil
- 1 teaspoon raspberry *or* seasoned rice vinegar
- Dash white pepper

Over small mixing bowl to catch juices section orange, reserving juice and orange sections separately. On serving platter arrange lettuce. Decoratively arrange jicama, orange sections, and scallion on lettuce; sprinkle with mint (or basil) and sunflower seed. Add remaining ingredients to reserved orange juice and, using a wire whisk, beat until thoroughly combined. Pour evenly over salad.

Each serving provides: 2½ Vegetable Exchanges; 1 Fat Exchange; ½ Fruit Exchange; 10 Optional Calories

Per serving: 104 calories; 2 g protein; 6 g fat; 13 g carbohydrate; 73 mg calcium; 7 mg sodium; 0 mg cholesterol; 3 g dietary fiber

Halibut Bake

Makes 2 servings

2 halibut fillets (3 ounces each)
¼ cup dry white table wine
1 tablespoon *each* chopped fresh dill,
   fresh basil, Italian (flat-leaf) parsley,
   and lemon juice

2 teaspoons minced shallot *or* onion
1 teaspoon olive *or* vegetable oil
1 garlic clove, sliced
⅛ teaspoon pepper

Set fish in single layer in 1½-quart casserole;* set aside. Using a fork, in small bowl combine remaining ingredients; pour over fish. Cover with plastic wrap and refrigerate overnight or at least 2 hours.

   Preheat oven to 425°F. Bake uncovered until fish flakes easily when tested with a fork, 5 to 6 minutes.

Each serving provides: 2 Protein Exchanges; ½ Fat Exchange; 30 Optional Calories

Per serving: 143 calories; 18 g protein; 4 g fat; 3 g carbohydrate; 69 mg calcium; 51 mg sodium; 27 mg cholesterol; 0.1 g dietary fiber

* It's best to marinate in glass or stainless-steel containers; acidic ingredients such as lemon juice may react with aluminum, causing color and flavor changes in foods.

WEIGHT RECIPE WATCHERS

Grilled Pineapple with Rum Butter

Makes 4 servings

Want to turn a fruit snack into something special? Try this delightful combination of flavors.

1 medium pineapple
2 tablespoons *each* **firmly packed light brown sugar and whipped butter**

1 tablespoon plus 1 teaspoon margarine
1 tablespoon dark rum

Cut pineapple in half crosswise (wrap half in plastic wrap and refrigerate for use at another time). Pare remaining pineapple half and cut crosswise into 8 equal slices (about ½-inch-thick each).

Preheat grill or broiler. Using a fork, in small mixing bowl combine sugar, butter, and margarine, mixing until smooth and creamy; continuing to stir, add rum, 1 teaspoon at a time, stirring until mixture is thoroughly combined.

Set pineapple slices on grill or on nonstick baking sheet and grill over hot coals (or broil), turning once, until lightly browned and heated through, 2 to 3 minutes on each side. Transfer pineapple slices to serving platter and immediately top each slice with ⅛ of the butter mixture (about 2 teaspoons). Let butter mixture melt, then serve.

Each serving provides: 1 Fat Exchange; 1 Fruit Exchange; 65 Optional Calories

Per serving: 125 calories; 0.3 g protein; 7 g fat; 15 g carbohydrate; 13 mg calcium; 76 mg sodium; 8 mg cholesterol; 1 g dietary fiber

JULY

SUNDAY	MONDAY	TUESDAY	WEDNESDAY
2	3	4	5
9	10	11	12
16	17	18	19
23 / 30	24 / 31	25	26

JULY

THURSDAY	FRIDAY	SATURDAY	NOTES/GOALS
		1	
6	7	8	
13	14	15	
20	21	22	
27	28	29	

WEEKLY FOOD DIARY

	MONDAY	TUESDAY	WEDNESDAY	THURSDAY	FRIDAY	SATURDAY	SUNDAY
BREAKFAST							
LUNCH							
DINNER							
SNACKS							
DAILY TOTALS	FRUIT ___ VEG ___ FAT ___ PROTEIN ___ BREAD ___ MILK ___ FLOATING ___	FRUIT ___ VEG ___ FAT ___ PROTEIN ___ BREAD ___ MILK ___ FLOATING ___	FRUIT ___ VEG ___ FAT ___ PROTEIN ___ BREAD ___ MILK ___ FLOATING ___	FRUIT ___ VEG ___ FAT ___ PROTEIN ___ BREAD ___ MILK ___ FLOATING ___	FRUIT ___ VEG ___ FAT ___ PROTEIN ___ BREAD ___ MILK ___ FLOATING ___	FRUIT ___ VEG ___ FAT ___ PROTEIN ___ BREAD ___ MILK ___ FLOATING ___	FRUIT ___ VEG ___ FAT ___ PROTEIN ___ BREAD ___ MILK ___ FLOATING ___

WEEKLY LIMITS EGGS ___ CHEESE ___ MEAT ___ ORGAN MEAT ___ OPTIONAL CALORIES ___

I will attend my Weight Watchers meeting this week on ___

JULY

1 9 8 9

MONDAY
3

Independence Day

TUESDAY
4

WEDNESDAY
5

THURSDAY
6

FRIDAY
7

SATURDAY
8

SUNDAY
9

	S	M	T	W	T	F	S
J						1	2	3
U	4	5	6	7	8	9	10
N	11	12	13	14	15	16	17
E	18	19	20	21	22	23	24
	25	26	27	28	29	30	

	S	M	T	W	T	F	S
J							1
U	2	3	4	5	6	7	8
L	9	10	11	12	13	14	15
Y	16	17	18	19	20	21	22
	23	24	25	26	27	28	29
	30	31					

	S	M	T	W	T	F	S
A		1	2	3	4	5
U	6	7	8	9	10	11	12
G	13	14	15	16	17	18	19
	20	21	22	23	24	25	26
	27	28	29	30	31		

WEEKLY FOOD DIARY

	MONDAY	TUESDAY	WEDNESDAY	THURSDAY	FRIDAY	SATURDAY	SUNDAY
BREAKFAST							
LUNCH							
DINNER							
SNACKS							
DAILY TOTALS	FRUIT ___ VEG ___ FAT ___ PROTEIN ___ BREAD ___ MILK ___ FLOATING ___	FRUIT ___ VEG ___ FAT ___ PROTEIN ___ BREAD ___ MILK ___ FLOATING ___	FRUIT ___ VEG ___ FAT ___ PROTEIN ___ BREAD ___ MILK ___ FLOATING ___	FRUIT ___ VEG ___ FAT ___ PROTEIN ___ BREAD ___ MILK ___ FLOATING ___	FRUIT ___ VEG ___ FAT ___ PROTEIN ___ BREAD ___ MILK ___ FLOATING ___	FRUIT ___ VEG ___ FAT ___ PROTEIN ___ BREAD ___ MILK ___ FLOATING ___	FRUIT ___ VEG ___ FAT ___ PROTEIN ___ BREAD ___ MILK ___ FLOATING ___

WEEKLY LIMITS   EGGS _____   CHEESE _____   MEAT _____   ORGAN MEAT _____   OPTIONAL CALORIES _____

I will attend my Weight Watchers meeting this week on _____

JULY

1 9 8 9

MONDAY
10

TUESDAY
11

WEDNESDAY
12

THURSDAY
13

FRIDAY
14

SATURDAY
15

SUNDAY
16

	S	M	T	W	T	F	S
JUNE					1	2	3
	4	5	6	7	8	9	10
	11	12	13	14	15	16	17
	18	19	20	21	22	23	24
	25	26	27	28	29	30	

	S	M	T	W	T	F	S
JULY							1
	2	3	4	5	6	7	8
	9	10	11	12	13	14	15
	16	17	18	19	20	21	22
	23	24	25	26	27	28	29
	30	31					

	S	M	T	W	T	F	S
AUG			1	2	3	4	5
	6	7	8	9	10	11	12
	13	14	15	16	17	18	19
	20	21	22	23	24	25	26
	27	28	29	30	31		

WEEKLY FOOD DIARY

	MONDAY	TUESDAY	WEDNESDAY	THURSDAY	FRIDAY	SATURDAY	SUNDAY
BREAKFAST							
LUNCH							
DINNER							
SNACKS							
DAILY TOTALS	FRUIT ____ VEG ____ FAT ____ PROTEIN ____ BREAD ____ MILK ____ FLOATING ____	FRUIT ____ VEG ____ FAT ____ PROTEIN ____ BREAD ____ MILK ____ FLOATING ____	FRUIT ____ VEG ____ FAT ____ PROTEIN ____ BREAD ____ MILK ____ FLOATING ____	FRUIT ____ VEG ____ FAT ____ PROTEIN ____ BREAD ____ MILK ____ FLOATING ____	FRUIT ____ VEG ____ FAT ____ PROTEIN ____ BREAD ____ MILK ____ FLOATING ____	FRUIT ____ VEG ____ FAT ____ PROTEIN ____ BREAD ____ MILK ____ FLOATING ____	FRUIT ____ VEG ____ FAT ____ PROTEIN ____ BREAD ____ MILK ____ FLOATING ____

WEEKLY LIMITS   EGGS _____   CHEESE _____   MEAT _____   ORGAN MEAT _____   OPTIONAL CALORIES _____

I will attend my Weight Watchers meeting this week on _____

MONDAY
17

TUESDAY
18

WEDNESDAY
19

THURSDAY
20

FRIDAY
21

SATURDAY
22

SUNDAY
23

	S	M	T	W	T	F	S
J						1	2	3
U	4	5	6	7	8	9	10
N	11	12	13	14	15	16	17
E	18	19	20	21	22	23	24
	25	26	27	28	29	30	

	S	M	T	W	T	F	S
J							1
U	2	3	4	5	6	7	8
L	9	10	11	12	13	14	15
Y	16	17	18	19	20	21	22
	23	24	25	26	27	28	29
	30	31					

	S	M	T	W	T	F	S
A		1	2	3	4	5
U	6	7	8	9	10	11	12
G	13	14	15	16	17	18	19
	20	21	22	23	24	25	26
	27	28	29	30	31		

WEEKLY FOOD DIARY

	MONDAY	TUESDAY	WEDNESDAY	THURSDAY	FRIDAY	SATURDAY	SUNDAY
BREAKFAST							
LUNCH							
DINNER							
SNACKS							
DAILY TOTALS	FRUIT ___ VEG ___ FAT ___ PROTEIN ___ BREAD ___ MILK ___ FLOATING ___	FRUIT ___ VEG ___ FAT ___ PROTEIN ___ BREAD ___ MILK ___ FLOATING ___	FRUIT ___ VEG ___ FAT ___ PROTEIN ___ BREAD ___ MILK ___ FLOATING ___	FRUIT ___ VEG ___ FAT ___ PROTEIN ___ BREAD ___ MILK ___ FLOATING ___	FRUIT ___ VEG ___ FAT ___ PROTEIN ___ BREAD ___ MILK ___ FLOATING ___	FRUIT ___ VEG ___ FAT ___ PROTEIN ___ BREAD ___ MILK ___ FLOATING ___	FRUIT ___ VEG ___ FAT ___ PROTEIN ___ BREAD ___ MILK ___ FLOATING ___

WEEKLY LIMITS   EGGS ___   CHEESE ___   MEAT ___   ORGAN MEAT ___   OPTIONAL CALORIES ___

I will attend my Weight Watchers meeting this week on ___

JULY

1 9 8 9

MONDAY
24

TUESDAY
25

WEDNESDAY
26

THURSDAY
27

FRIDAY
28

SATURDAY
29

SUNDAY
30

	S	M	T	W	T	F	S
					1	2	3
J	4	5	6	7	8	9	10
U	11	12	13	14	15	16	17
N	18	19	20	21	22	23	24
E	25	26	27	28	29	30	

	S	M	T	W	T	F	S
							1
J	2	3	4	5	6	7	8
U	9	10	11	12	13	14	15
L	16	17	18	19	20	21	22
Y	23	24	25	26	27	28	29
	30	31					

	S	M	T	W	T	F	S
			1	2	3	4	5
A	6	7	8	9	10	11	12
U	13	14	15	16	17	18	19
G	20	21	22	23	24	25	26
	27	28	29	30	31		

Mango-Peach Daiquiri

Makes 2 servings, about 1½ cups each

Get a taste of the tropics in this luscious drink.

1 small mango, pared, pitted, and sliced
1 medium peach (about ¼ pound),
  blanched, peeled, pitted, and sliced
¼ cup light rum
2 tablespoons freshly squeezed lime
  juice

1 tablespoon lemon juice
1½ teaspoons superfine sugar*
9 ice cubes
Garnish: 2 mint sprigs

Chill two 12-ounce glasses. In blender container combine all ingredients except ice cubes and garnish and process until smooth; with motor running add ice cubes, 1 at a time, processing after each addition until all ice is dissolved (mixture will be thick and smooth). Pour half of mixture into each chilled glass and garnish each with a mint sprig.

Each serving provides: 1½ Fruit Exchanges; 90 Optional Calories

Per serving: 167 calories; 1 g protein; 0.3 g fat; 27 g carbohydrate; 15 mg calcium; 4 mg sodium; 0 mg cholesterol; 1 g dietary fiber

* If superfine sugar is not available, process granulated sugar in blender container until superfine.

Kiwi Ice

Makes 4 servings, about ½ cup each

¾ cup water
3 tablespoons *each* **granulated sugar
and light corn syrup**

1 tablespoon lemon juice
½ teaspoon grated orange peel
¾ pound kiwi fruit, pared and pureed

In 1-quart saucepan combine all ingredients except kiwi fruit. Cook over high heat, stirring occasionally, until mixture comes to a boil; continue cooking, stirring frequently, for 2 minutes. Transfer sugar mixture to medium mixing bowl; stir in kiwi puree until thoroughly combined. Pour mixture into a 12 × 9 × 2-inch freezer-safe container (not aluminum*); cover with plastic wrap and freeze until partially frozen, about 1 hour. Transfer kiwi mixture to medium mixing bowl and, using electric mixer, beat at low speed until light and fluffy. Cover with plastic wrap and freeze until firm, 1 to 2 hours.

To serve, scoop into 4 dessert dishes.

Each serving provides: 1 Fruit Exchange; 90 Optional Calories

Per serving: 127 calories; 0.7 g protein; 0.3 g fat; 32 g carbohydrate; 27 mg calcium; 15 mg sodium; 0 mg cholesterol; 0 g dietary fiber

* It's best not to freeze in an aluminum container since aluminum may react with the ice, causing flavor changes.

Pesto Toasts

Makes 8 servings, 2 toasts each

Serve warm pesto toast as an appetizer or hors d'oeuvre when guests come, or treat yourself to this Italian classic.

1 cup firmly packed basil leaves
¼ cup firmly packed Italian (flat-leaf) parsley
1 ounce pignolia nuts (pine nuts), reserve 16 nuts for garnish
2 tablespoons plus 2 teaspoons *each* grated Parmesan cheese and olive oil

1 garlic clove, crushed
¼ teaspoon salt
16 slices French bread (½ ounce each), toasted

In work bowl of food processor fitted with steel blade combine all ingredients except reserved pignolia nuts and French bread. Using on-off motion process mixture until basil and parsley are coarsely chopped, about 1 minute, then process continuously for 1 minute. Scrape down sides of container and process until mixture is thoroughly combined and pureed, about 1 minute longer.

On baking sheet place toasted bread slices and spread an equal amount of basil mixture (about 1 teaspoon) over each; set 1 reserved nut in center of each toast slice. Broil until pesto is heated through, about 2 minutes.

Each serving provide: 1 Bread Exchange; 1 Fat Exchange; 40 Optional Calories

Per serving: 157 calories; 5 g protein; 8 g fat; 18 g carbohydrate; 103 mg calcium; 265 mg sodium; 2 mg cholesterol; 0.9 g dietary fiber*

Variation: For a more robust flavor, substitute grated Romano cheese for the Parmesan cheese.

Per serving: 156 calories; 4 g protein; 8 g fat; 18 g carbohydrate; 98 mg calcium, 254 mg sodium; 3 g cholesterol; 0.9 g dietary fiber*

* This figure does not include pine nuts; nutrition analysis not available.

Crabmeat Salad

Makes 2 servings

¼ pound thawed and drained frozen crabmeat

½ cup *each* pared, seeded, and diced cucumber and diced celery

2 tablespoons *each* finely diced red onion and reduced-calorie mayonnaise

1 tablespoon *each* minced fresh dill and freshly squeezed lemon *or* lime juice

⅛ teaspoon salt

Dash white pepper

8 lettuce leaves

1 medium tomato, cut into wedges

Garnish: lemon *or* lime slices and dill sprigs

In medium mixing bowl combine all ingredients except lettuce, tomato, and garnish, mixing until combined. Cover with plastic wrap and refrigerate until ready to use.

To serve, line each of 2 chilled salad plates with 4 lettuce leaves; top each portion of lettuce with half of the crab mixture. Around each portion of crab mixture arrange half of the tomato wedges; garnish salad with lemon or lime slices and dill.

Each serving provides: 2 Protein Exchanges; 3⅛ Vegetable Exchanges; 1½ Fat Exchanges

Per serving:168 calories; 16 g protein; 6 g fat; 16 g carbohydrate; 246 mg calcium; 464 mg sodium; 62 mg cholesterol; 6 g dietary fiber

AUGUST

SUNDAY	MONDAY	TUESDAY	WEDNESDAY
		1	2
6	7	8	9
13	14	15	16
20	21	22	23
27	28	29	30

AUGUST

THURSDAY	FRIDAY	SATURDAY	NOTES/GOALS
3	4	5	
10	11	12	
17	18	19	
24	25	26	
31			

WEEKLY FOOD DIARY

	MONDAY	TUESDAY	WEDNESDAY	THURSDAY	FRIDAY	SATURDAY	SUNDAY
BREAKFAST							
LUNCH							
DINNER							
SNACKS							
DAILY TOTALS	FRUIT ____ VEG ____ FAT ____ PROTEIN ____ BREAD ____ MILK ____ FLOATING ____	FRUIT ____ VEG ____ FAT ____ PROTEIN ____ BREAD ____ MILK ____ FLOATING ____	FRUIT ____ VEG ____ FAT ____ PROTEIN ____ BREAD ____ MILK ____ FLOATING ____	FRUIT ____ VEG ____ FAT ____ PROTEIN ____ BREAD ____ MILK ____ FLOATING ____	FRUIT ____ VEG ____ FAT ____ PROTEIN ____ BREAD ____ MILK ____ FLOATING ____	FRUIT ____ VEG ____ FAT ____ PROTEIN ____ BREAD ____ MILK ____ FLOATING ____	FRUIT ____ VEG ____ FAT ____ PROTEIN ____ BREAD ____ MILK ____ FLOATING ____

WEEKLY LIMITS EGGS ____ CHEESE ____ MEAT ____ ORGAN MEAT ____ OPTIONAL CALORIES ____

I will attend my Weight Watchers meeting this week on ____

JULY
AUGUST

1989

MONDAY
31

TUESDAY
1

WEDNESDAY
2

THURSDAY
3

FRIDAY
4

SATURDAY
5

SUNDAY
6

	S	M	T	W	T	F	S
							1
J	2	3	4	5	6	7	8
U	9	10	11	12	13	14	15
L	16	17	18	19	20	21	22
Y	23	24	25	26	27	28	29
	30	31					

	S	M	T	W	T	F	S
			1	2	3	4	5
A	6	7	8	9	10	11	12
U	13	14	15	16	17	18	19
G	20	21	22	23	24	25	26
	27	28	29	30	31		

	S	M	T	W	T	F	S
						1	2
S	3	4	5	6	7	8	9
E	10	11	12	13	14	15	16
P	17	18	19	20	21	22	23
T	24	25	26	27	28	29	30

WEEKLY FOOD DIARY

	MONDAY	TUESDAY	WEDNESDAY	THURSDAY	FRIDAY	SATURDAY	SUNDAY
BREAKFAST							
LUNCH							
DINNER							
SNACKS							
DAILY TOTALS	FRUIT ___ VEG ___ FAT ___ PROTEIN ___ BREAD ___ MILK ___ FLOATING ___	FRUIT ___ VEG ___ FAT ___ PROTEIN ___ BREAD ___ MILK ___ FLOATING ___	FRUIT ___ VEG ___ FAT ___ PROTEIN ___ BREAD ___ MILK ___ FLOATING ___	FRUIT ___ VEG ___ FAT ___ PROTEIN ___ BREAD ___ MILK ___ FLOATING ___	FRUIT ___ VEG ___ FAT ___ PROTEIN ___ BREAD ___ MILK ___ FLOATING ___	FRUIT ___ VEG ___ FAT ___ PROTEIN ___ BREAD ___ MILK ___ FLOATING ___	FRUIT ___ VEG ___ FAT ___ PROTEIN ___ BREAD ___ MILK ___ FLOATING ___

WEEKLY LIMITS   EGGS ___   CHEESE ___   MEAT ___   ORGAN MEAT ___   OPTIONAL CALORIES ___

I will attend my Weight Watchers meeting this week on ___

AUGUST

MONDAY
7

TUESDAY
8

WEDNESDAY
9

THURSDAY
10

FRIDAY
11

SATURDAY
12

SUNDAY
13

	S	M	T	W	T	F	S
							1
J	2	3	4	5	6	7	8
U	9	10	11	12	13	14	15
L	16	17	18	19	20	21	22
Y	23	24	25	26	27	28	29
	30	31					

	S	M	T	W	T	F	S
			1	2	3	4	5
A	6	7	8	9	10	11	12
U	13	14	15	16	17	18	19
G	20	21	22	23	24	25	26
	27	28	29	30	31		

	S	M	T	W	T	F	S
S						1	2
E	3	4	5	6	7	8	9
P	10	11	12	13	14	15	16
T	17	18	19	20	21	22	23
	24	25	26	27	28	29	30

WEEKLY FOOD DIARY

	MONDAY	TUESDAY	WEDNESDAY	THURSDAY	FRIDAY	SATURDAY	SUNDAY
BREAKFAST							
LUNCH							
DINNER							
SNACKS							
DAILY TOTALS	FRUIT _____ VEG _____ FAT _____ PROTEIN _____ BREAD _____ MILK _____ FLOATING _____	FRUIT _____ VEG _____ FAT _____ PROTEIN _____ BREAD _____ MILK _____ FLOATING _____	FRUIT _____ VEG _____ FAT _____ PROTEIN _____ BREAD _____ MILK _____ FLOATING _____	FRUIT _____ VEG _____ FAT _____ PROTEIN _____ BREAD _____ MILK _____ FLOATING _____	FRUIT _____ VEG _____ FAT _____ PROTEIN _____ BREAD _____ MILK _____ FLOATING _____	FRUIT _____ VEG _____ FAT _____ PROTEIN _____ BREAD _____ MILK _____ FLOATING _____	FRUIT _____ VEG _____ FAT _____ PROTEIN _____ BREAD _____ MILK _____ FLOATING _____

WEEKLY LIMITS   EGGS _____   CHEESE _____   MEAT _____   ORGAN MEAT _____   OPTIONAL CALORIES _____

I will attend my Weight Watchers meeting this week on _____

MONDAY
14

TUESDAY
15

WEDNESDAY
16

THURSDAY
17

FRIDAY
18

SATURDAY
19

SUNDAY
20

	S	M	T	W	T	F	S
							1
J	2	3	4	5	6	7	8
U	9	10	11	12	13	14	15
L	16	17	18	19	20	21	22
Y	23	24	25	26	27	28	29
	30	31					

	S	M	T	W	T	F	S
			1	2	3	4	5
A	6	7	8	9	10	11	12
U	13	14	15	16	17	18	19
G	20	21	22	23	24	25	26
	27	28	29	30	31		

	S	M	T	W	T	F	S
						1	2
S	3	4	5	6	7	8	9
E	10	11	12	13	14	15	16
P	17	18	19	20	21	22	23
T	24	25	26	27	28	29	30

WEEKLY FOOD DIARY

	MONDAY	TUESDAY	WEDNESDAY	THURSDAY	FRIDAY	SATURDAY	SUNDAY
BREAKFAST							
LUNCH							
DINNER							
SNACKS							
DAILY TOTALS	FRUIT _____ VEG _____ FAT _____ PROTEIN _____ BREAD _____ MILK _____ FLOATING _____	FRUIT _____ VEG _____ FAT _____ PROTEIN _____ BREAD _____ MILK _____ FLOATING _____	FRUIT _____ VEG _____ FAT _____ PROTEIN _____ BREAD _____ MILK _____ FLOATING _____	FRUIT _____ VEG _____ FAT _____ PROTEIN _____ BREAD _____ MILK _____ FLOATING _____	FRUIT _____ VEG _____ FAT _____ PROTEIN _____ BREAD _____ MILK _____ FLOATING _____	FRUIT _____ VEG _____ FAT _____ PROTEIN _____ BREAD _____ MILK _____ FLOATING _____	FRUIT _____ VEG _____ FAT _____ PROTEIN _____ BREAD _____ MILK _____ FLOATING _____

WEEKLY LIMITS   EGGS _____   CHEESE _____   MEAT _____   ORGAN MEAT _____   OPTIONAL CALORIES _____

I will attend my Weight Watchers meeting this week on _____

AUGUST

MONDAY
21

TUESDAY
22

WEDNESDAY
23

THURSDAY
24

FRIDAY
25

SATURDAY
26

SUNDAY
27

	S	M	T	W	T	F	S
							1
J	2	3	4	5	6	7	8
U	9	10	11	12	13	14	15
L	16	17	18	19	20	21	22
Y	23	24	25	26	27	28	29
	30	31					

	S	M	T	W	T	F	S
			1	2	3	4	5
A	6	7	8	9	10	11	12
U	13	14	15	16	17	18	19
G	20	21	22	23	24	25	26
	27	28	29	30	31		

	S	M	T	W	T	F	S
S						1	2
E	3	4	5	6	7	8	9
P	10	11	12	13	14	15	16
T	17	18	19	20	21	22	23
	24	25	26	27	28	29	30

WEEKLY FOOD DIARY

	MONDAY	TUESDAY	WEDNESDAY	THURSDAY	FRIDAY	SATURDAY	SUNDAY
BREAKFAST							
LUNCH							
DINNER							
SNACKS							
DAILY TOTALS	FRUIT ___ VEG ___ FAT ___ PROTEIN ___ BREAD ___ MILK ___ FLOATING ___	FRUIT ___ VEG ___ FAT ___ PROTEIN ___ BREAD ___ MILK ___ FLOATING ___	FRUIT ___ VEG ___ FAT ___ PROTEIN ___ BREAD ___ MILK ___ FLOATING ___	FRUIT ___ VEG ___ FAT ___ PROTEIN ___ BREAD ___ MILK ___ FLOATING ___	FRUIT ___ VEG ___ FAT ___ PROTEIN ___ BREAD ___ MILK ___ FLOATING ___	FRUIT ___ VEG ___ FAT ___ PROTEIN ___ BREAD ___ MILK ___ FLOATING ___	FRUIT ___ VEG ___ FAT ___ PROTEIN ___ BREAD ___ MILK ___ FLOATING ___

WEEKLY LIMITS   EGGS _____   CHEESE _____   MEAT _____   ORGAN MEAT _____   OPTIONAL CALORIES _____

I will attend my Weight Watchers meeting this week on _____

AUGUST
SEPTEMBER

1 9 8 9

MONDAY
28

TUESDAY
29

WEDNESDAY
30

THURSDAY
31

FRIDAY
1

SATURDAY
2

SUNDAY
3

	S	M	T	W	T	F	S
							1
J	2	3	4	5	6	7	8
U	9	10	11	12	13	14	15
L	16	17	18	19	20	21	22
Y	23	24	25	26	27	28	29
	30	31					

	S	M	T	W	T	F	S
			1	2	3	4	5
A	6	7	8	9	10	11	12
U	13	14	15	16	17	18	19
G	20	21	22	23	24	25	26
	27	28	29	30	31		

	S	M	T	W	T	F	S
						1	2
S	3	4	5	6	7	8	9
E	10	11	12	13	14	15	16
P	17	18	19	20	21	22	23
T	24	25	26	27	28	29	30

WEIGHT

RECIPE

WATCHERS

Grilled Swordfish with Lime Butter

Makes 2 servings

2 boneless swordfish steaks (3 ounces each)
1 tablespoon plus 1 teaspoon freshly squeezed lime juice, divided

1 teaspoon chopped fresh mint
1 tablespoon whipped butter, softened
2 teaspoons margarine
¼ teaspoon grated lime peel

Set fish in single layer in shallow container (not aluminum*). In cup or small bowl combine 1 tablespoon lime juice and the mint; pour over fish. Cover with plastic wrap and refrigerate for 15 minutes.

Preheat grill or broiler. Using a fork, in small mixing bowl combine butter and margarine, mixing until light and fluffy; add remaining teaspoon lime juice and the lime peel and mix until thoroughly combined. Cover with plastic wrap and refrigerate until ready to use.

Remove fish from marinade. Set fish on grill or on rack in broiling pan and grill over hot coals (or broil) for 2 to 4 minutes, depending on thickness of steaks. Carefully turn fish over and cook until fish flakes easily when tested with a fork, 2 to 4 minutes longer. Transfer fish to serving platter and immediately top with half of the butter mixture.

Each serving provides: 2 Protein Exchanges; 1 Fat Exchange; 25 Optional Calories

Per serving: 200 calories; 23 g protein; 11 g fat; 1 g carbohydrate; 8 mg calcium; 176 mg sodium; 52 mg cholesterol; 0 g dietary fiber

* It's best to marinate in glass or stainless-steel containers; acidic ingredients such as lemon juice may react with aluminum, causing color and flavor changes in foods.

Mixed Fruit Mélange

Makes 4 servings

This elegant appetizer or snack can be prepared 1 to 2 hours in advance. Serve at room temperature.

1½ cups honeydew *or* cantaloupe
   chunks *or* balls
1 cup strawberries
1 medium peach (about 4 ounces),
   blanched, peeled, pitted, and sliced
¼ cup freshly squeezed orange juice

1 tablespoon *each* orange liqueur and
   freshly squeezed lime juice
1 teaspoon chopped fresh mint
¼ teaspoon grated orange peel
Garnish: 4 mint sprigs

In large glass or stainless-steel bowl (not aluminum*) combine all ingredients except garnish. Let stand at room temperature until flavors blend, about 10 minutes. Into each of 4 dessert dishes or champagne glasses spoon ¼ of the fruit. Garnish each portion with a mint sprig and serve.

Each serving provides: 1 Fruit Exchange; 15 Optional Calories

Per serving with honeydew: 61 calories; 0.8 g protein; 0.2 g fat; 14 g carbohydrate; 13 mg calcium; 7 mg sodium; 0 mg cholesterol; 1 g dietary fiber

With cantaloupe: 60 calories; 1 g protein; 0.3 g fat; 13 g carbohydrate; 15 mg calcium; 6 mg sodium; 0 mg cholesterol; 1 g dietary fiber

* It's best to marinate in glass or stainless-steel containers; acidic ingredients such as lime juice may react with aluminum, causing color and flavor changes in foods.

Warm Sausage and Pasta Salad

Makes 2 servings

This salad makes a hearty first course or an excellent light meal.

2 teaspoons olive oil, divided
5 ounces veal sausage, cut into ½-inch-thick slices
½ cup diced onion
1 to 2 small garlic cloves, mashed
1 cup cooked ziti macaroni
½ cup *each* diced red bell pepper and celery

2 tablespoons *each* balsamic *or* cider vinegar and chopped fresh basil
⅛ teaspoon *each* oregano leaves and fennel seed
Dash *each* salt and pepper
4 lettuce leaves
½ medium tomato, sliced
Garnish: fresh basil leaves

In 10-inch skillet heat 1 teaspoon oil; add sausage, onion, and garlic and cook, stirring occasionally, until sausage is lightly browned, 10 to 15 minutes. Transfer to medium mixing bowl; add macaroni, bell pepper, celery, vinegar, remaining teaspoon oil, and the seasonings and stir to combine. Line serving platter with lettuce leaves; top with sausage mixture. Arrange tomato slices around sausage mixture and garnish with basil.

Each serving provides: 2 Protein Exchanges; 1 Bread Exchange; 2½ Vegetable Exchanges; 1 Fat Exchange

Per serving: 292 calories; 20 g protein; 12 g fat; 25 g carbohydrate; 74 mg calcium; 860 mg sodium; 57 mg cholesterol; 2 g dietary fiber

Scallop Appetizer with Jalapeño Butter

Makes 4 servings

Any firm white fish may be substituted for the scallops.

¼ cup whipped butter
1 tablespoon plus 1 teaspoon sour cream
2 teaspoons seeded and minced jalapeño pepper

1 teaspoon freshly squeezed lime juice
Dash white pepper
5 ounces bay scallops (or sea scallops, cut into ½-inch pieces)

In work bowl of food processor fitted with steel blade or blender container process butter until smooth and creamy; add remaining ingredients except scallops and continue processing, scraping down sides of container as necessary, until mixture is thoroughly combined. Set aside.

Preheat broiler. Onto each of 4 flameproof medium scallop shells arrange ¼ of the scallops; top each portion with ¼ of the butter mixture. Broil until scallops are lightly browned, 3 to 4 minutes.

Each serving provides: 1 Protein Exchange; 60 Optional Calories

Per serving: 93 calories; 6 g protein; 7 g fat; 1 g carbohydrate; 16 g calcium; 118 mg sodium; 29 mg cholesterol; trace dietary fiber

SEPTEMBER

SUNDAY	MONDAY	TUESDAY	WEDNESDAY
3	4	5	6
10	11	12	13
17	18	19	20
24	25	26	27

SEPTEMBER

THURSDAY	FRIDAY	SATURDAY	NOTES/GOALS
	1	2	
7	8	9	
14	15	16	
21	22	23	
28	29	30	

WEEKLY FOOD DIARY

	MONDAY	TUESDAY	WEDNESDAY	THURSDAY	FRIDAY	SATURDAY	SUNDAY
BREAKFAST							
LUNCH							
DINNER							
SNACKS							
DAILY TOTALS	FRUIT ___ VEG ___ FAT ___ PROTEIN ___ BREAD ___ MILK ___ FLOATING ___	FRUIT ___ VEG ___ FAT ___ PROTEIN ___ BREAD ___ MILK ___ FLOATING ___	FRUIT ___ VEG ___ FAT ___ PROTEIN ___ BREAD ___ MILK ___ FLOATING ___	FRUIT ___ VEG ___ FAT ___ PROTEIN ___ BREAD ___ MILK ___ FLOATING ___	FRUIT ___ VEG ___ FAT ___ PROTEIN ___ BREAD ___ MILK ___ FLOATING ___	FRUIT ___ VEG ___ FAT ___ PROTEIN ___ BREAD ___ MILK ___ FLOATING ___	FRUIT ___ VEG ___ FAT ___ PROTEIN ___ BREAD ___ MILK ___ FLOATING ___

WEEKLY LIMITS   EGGS ___   CHEESE ___   MEAT ___   ORGAN MEAT ___   OPTIONAL CALORIES ___

I will attend my Weight Watchers meeting this week on ___

SEPTEMBER

1 9 8 9

Labor Day

MONDAY
4

TUESDAY
5

WEDNESDAY
6

THURSDAY
7

FRIDAY
8

SATURDAY
9

SUNDAY
10

	S	M	T	W	T	F	S
			1	2	3	4	5
A	6	7	8	9	10	11	12
U	13	14	15	16	17	18	19
G	20	21	22	23	24	25	26
	27	28	29	30	31		

	S	M	T	W	T	F	S
						1	2
S	3	4	5	6	7	8	9
E	10	11	12	13	14	15	16
P	17	18	19	20	21	22	23
T	24	25	26	27	28	29	30

	S	M	T	W	T	F	S
	1	2	3	4	5	6	7
O	8	9	10	11	12	13	14
C	15	16	17	18	19	20	21
T	22	23	24	25	26	27	28
	29	30	31				

WEEKLY FOOD DIARY

	MONDAY	TUESDAY	WEDNESDAY	THURSDAY	FRIDAY	SATURDAY	SUNDAY
BREAKFAST							
LUNCH							
DINNER							
SNACKS							
DAILY TOTALS	FRUIT ___ VEG ___ FAT ___ PROTEIN ___ BREAD ___ MILK ___ FLOATING ___	FRUIT ___ VEG ___ FAT ___ PROTEIN ___ BREAD ___ MILK ___ FLOATING ___	FRUIT ___ VEG ___ FAT ___ PROTEIN ___ BREAD ___ MILK ___ FLOATING ___	FRUIT ___ VEG ___ FAT ___ PROTEIN ___ BREAD ___ MILK ___ FLOATING ___	FRUIT ___ VEG ___ FAT ___ PROTEIN ___ BREAD ___ MILK ___ FLOATING ___	FRUIT ___ VEG ___ FAT ___ PROTEIN ___ BREAD ___ MILK ___ FLOATING ___	FRUIT ___ VEG ___ FAT ___ PROTEIN ___ BREAD ___ MILK ___ FLOATING ___

WEEKLY LIMITS   EGGS _____   CHEESE _____   MEAT _____   ORGAN MEAT _____   OPTIONAL CALORIES _____

I will attend my Weight Watchers meeting this week on _____

ENGAGEMENTS

SEPTEMBER

1989

MONDAY
11

TUESDAY
12

WEDNESDAY
13

THURSDAY
14

FRIDAY
15

SATURDAY
16

SUNDAY
17

	S	M	T	W	T	F	S
			1	2	3	4	5
A	6	7	8	9	10	11	12
U	13	14	15	16	17	18	19
G	20	21	22	23	24	25	26
	27	28	29	30	31		

	S	M	T	W	T	F	S
						1	2
S	3	4	5	6	7	8	9
E	10	11	12	13	14	15	16
P	17	18	19	20	21	22	23
T	24	25	26	27	28	29	30

	S	M	T	W	T	F	S
	1	2	3	4	5	6	7
O	8	9	10	11	12	13	14
C	15	16	17	18	19	20	21
T	22	23	24	25	26	27	28
	29	30	31				

WEEKLY FOOD DIARY

	MONDAY	TUESDAY	WEDNESDAY	THURSDAY	FRIDAY	SATURDAY	SUNDAY
BREAKFAST							
LUNCH							
DINNER							
SNACKS							
DAILY TOTALS	FRUIT ___ VEG ___ FAT ___ PROTEIN ___ BREAD ___ MILK ___ FLOATING ___	FRUIT ___ VEG ___ FAT ___ PROTEIN ___ BREAD ___ MILK ___ FLOATING ___	FRUIT ___ VEG ___ FAT ___ PROTEIN ___ BREAD ___ MILK ___ FLOATING ___	FRUIT ___ VEG ___ FAT ___ PROTEIN ___ BREAD ___ MILK ___ FLOATING ___	FRUIT ___ VEG ___ FAT ___ PROTEIN ___ BREAD ___ MILK ___ FLOATING ___	FRUIT ___ VEG ___ FAT ___ PROTEIN ___ BREAD ___ MILK ___ FLOATING ___	FRUIT ___ VEG ___ FAT ___ PROTEIN ___ BREAD ___ MILK ___ FLOATING ___

WEEKLY LIMITS EGGS _____ CHEESE _____ MEAT _____ ORGAN MEAT _____ OPTIONAL CALORIES _____

I will attend my Weight Watchers meeting this week on _____

MONDAY
18

TUESDAY
19

WEDNESDAY
20

THURSDAY
21

FRIDAY
22

SATURDAY
23

SUNDAY
24

	S	M	T	W	T	F	S
			1	2	3	4	5
A	6	7	8	9	10	11	12
U	13	14	15	16	17	18	19
G	20	21	22	23	24	25	26
	27	28	29	30	31		

	S	M	T	W	T	F	S
						1	2
S	3	4	5	6	7	8	9
E	10	11	12	13	14	15	16
P	17	18	19	20	21	22	23
T	24	25	26	27	28	29	30

	S	M	T	W	T	F	S
	1	2	3	4	5	6	7
O	8	9	10	11	12	13	14
C	15	16	17	18	19	20	21
T	22	23	24	25	26	27	28
	29	30	31				

WEEKLY FOOD DIARY

	MONDAY	TUESDAY	WEDNESDAY	THURSDAY	FRIDAY	SATURDAY	SUNDAY
BREAKFAST							
LUNCH							
DINNER							
SNACKS							
DAILY TOTALS	FRUIT ___ VEG ___ FAT ___ PROTEIN ___ BREAD ___ MILK ___ FLOATING ___	FRUIT ___ VEG ___ FAT ___ PROTEIN ___ BREAD ___ MILK ___ FLOATING ___	FRUIT ___ VEG ___ FAT ___ PROTEIN ___ BREAD ___ MILK ___ FLOATING ___	FRUIT ___ VEG ___ FAT ___ PROTEIN ___ BREAD ___ MILK ___ FLOATING ___	FRUIT ___ VEG ___ FAT ___ PROTEIN ___ BREAD ___ MILK ___ FLOATING ___	FRUIT ___ VEG ___ FAT ___ PROTEIN ___ BREAD ___ MILK ___ FLOATING ___	FRUIT ___ VEG ___ FAT ___ PROTEIN ___ BREAD ___ MILK ___ FLOATING ___

WEEKLY LIMITS EGGS ___ CHEESE ___ MEAT ___ ORGAN MEAT ___ OPTIONAL CALORIES ___

I will attend my Weight Watchers meeting this week on ___

MONDAY
25

TUESDAY
26

WEDNESDAY
27

THURSDAY
28

FRIDAY
29

First Day of Rosh Hashanah

SATURDAY
30

SUNDAY
1

	S	M	T	W	T	F	S
			1	2	3	4	5
A	6	7	8	9	10	11	12
U	13	14	15	16	17	18	19
G	20	21	22	23	24	25	26
	27	28	29	30	31		

	S	M	T	W	T	F	S
						1	2
S	3	4	5	6	7	8	9
E	10	11	12	13	14	15	16
P	17	18	19	20	21	22	23
T	24	25	26	27	28	29	30

	S	M	T	W	T	F	S
	1	2	3	4	5	6	7
O	8	9	10	11	12	13	14
C	15	16	17	18	19	20	21
T	22	23	24	25	26	27	28
	29	30	31				

WEIGHT
RECIPE
WATCHERS

Cream of Tomato-Vegetable Soup

Makes 4 servings, about 1 cup each

Store soup in serving-size portions in freezer for future use.

2 teaspoons margarine
½ cup *each* diced onion, carrot, and celery
1 small garlic clove, minced
1 packet instant chicken broth and seasoning mix
2 teaspoons all-purpose flour

1½ cups water
1 cup canned Italian tomatoes (with liquid); drain, seed, and chop tomatoes, reserving liquid
⅓ cup half-and-half (blend of milk and cream)

In 2-quart saucepan melt margarine; add onion, carrot, celery, and garlic and cook, stirring occasionally, until vegetables are tender-crisp, 2 to 3 minutes. Sprinkle broth mix and flour over vegetable mixture in saucepan and stir quickly to combine; cook, stirring constantly, for 1 minute. Gradually stir in water; add tomatoes and reserved liquid, stir to combine, and bring to a boil. Reduce heat to low and let simmer until flavors blend, about 10 minutes. Remove saucepan from heat; stir in half-and-half. Return to low heat and let simmer until heated through, 1 to 2 minutes.

Each serving provides: 1¼ Vegetable Exchanges; ½ Fat Exchange; 40 Optional Calories

Per serving: 79 calories; 2 g protein; 4 g fat; 9 g carbohydrate; 53 mg calcium; 396 mg sodium; 7 mg cholesterol; 1 g dietary fiber

Pasta with Chicken 'n' Tomatoes

Makes 2 servings

2 tablespoons whipped butter
1 tablespoon olive oil
5 ounces skinned and boned chicken
   breast, cut into 3 × ½-inch strips
½ cup sliced shiitake mushrooms*
2 garlic cloves, minced
¾ cup canned ready-to-serve chicken
   broth

2 medium tomatoes, skinned, seeded,
   and cut into strips
2 tablespoons chopped fresh basil
Dash pepper
1 cup cooked fettuccine (hot)
1 tablespoon grated Parmesan cheese

In 10-inch nonstick skillet combine butter and oil and heat until butter is melted; add chicken, mushrooms, and garlic and sauté over medium-high heat, stirring occasionally, until chicken is lightly browned, 2 to 3 minutes.

   Pour broth into skillet and stir well to combine. Reduce heat to medium; add tomatoes, basil, and pepper to skillet and stir to combine. Add fettuccine and, using 2 forks, toss thoroughly to coat with sauce. Transfer pasta and chicken mixture to serving bowl; sprinkle with Parmesan cheese and serve.

Each serving provides: 2 Protein Exchanges; 1 Bread Exchange; 2½ Vegetable Exchanges; 1½ Fat Exchanges; 80 Optional Calories

Per serving: 325 calories; 22 g protein; 16 g fat; 25 g carbohydrate; 88 mg calcium; 540 mg sodium; 59 mg cholesterol; 2 g dietary fiber

* Regular mushrooms may be substituted for the shiitake mushrooms.

Variation: Substitute 4 sun-dried tomato halves (not packed in oil) for the fresh tomatoes. Before beginning to sauté chicken and mushrooms, bring the chicken broth to a boil; add sun-dried tomatoes, remove pan from heat, and let stand until tomatoes are plumped. Cut plumped tomatoes into long, thin strips and proceed as directed. Reduce Vegetable Exchange to 1½ Exchanges.

Per serving: 325 calories; 22 g protein; 16 g fat; 25 g carbohydrate; 88 mg calcium; 810 mg sodium (estimated); 59 mg cholesterol; 2 g dietary fiber

WEIGHT RECIPE WATCHERS

Chocolate Cupcakes

Makes 4 servings, 2 cupcakes each

Yes, you really can make light and delicious cupcakes without any flour. Try these and you'll see!

2 eggs (at room temperature)
¼ cup granulated sugar
1 teaspoon vanilla extract

2 tablespoons unsweetened cocoa,
sifted

Preheat oven to 350°F. Line eight 2½-inch-diameter muffin pan cups with paper baking cups; set aside.

Using electric mixer at medium-high speed, in medium mixing bowl beat eggs until light and fluffy and double in volume, 3 to 4 minutes. Gradually add sugar, one tablespoon at a time, beating after each addition until blended. Stir in vanilla. Sprinkle cocoa over batter and fold in. Divide batter evenly into baking cups (each cup will be about ⅔ full). Partially fill empty cups with water (this will prevent pan from burning and/or warping). Bake in middle of center oven rack until a toothpick, inserted in center of cupcake, comes out clean, about 20 minutes. Remove cupcakes to wire rack and let cool.

Each serving provides: ½ Protein Exchange; 70 Optional Calories

Per serving: 98 calories; 3 g protein; 3 g fat; 14 g carbohydrate; 17 mg calcium; 35 mg sodium; 137 mg cholesterol; 0 g dietary fiber

Open-Face Dilly Crab Sandwiches

Makes 2 servings, 2 open-face sandwiches each

A terrific hors d'oeuvre idea.

**2 ounces thawed and thoroughly
drained frozen crabmeat, chilled
1 tablespoon plus 1 teaspoon reduced-
calorie mayonnaise
1 tablespoon sour cream
1 teaspoon chopped fresh dill
½ teaspoon *each* lemon juice and Dijon
mustard**

**¼ teaspoon grated lemon peel
4 slices pumpernickel cocktail bread
(1½ ounces)
2 lettuce leaves, cut into halves
Garnish: 2 lemon slices, halved, and 4
dill sprigs**

In small mixing bowl combine crabmeat, mayonnaise, sour cream, dill, lemon juice, mustard, and lemon peel and stir until thoroughly combined.

Top each slice of bread with a lettuce leaf half and then spread ¼ of crab mixture over each. Top each portion with lemon slice and dill sprig.

Each serving provides: 1 Protein Exchange; 1 Bread Exchange; ¼ Vegetable Exchange; 1 Fat Exchange; 15 Optional Calories

Per serving: 129 calories; 8 g protein; 5 g fat; 13 g carbohydrate; 69 mg calcium; 318 mg sodium; 35 mg cholesterol; 0.4 g dietary fiber

OCTOBER

SUNDAY	MONDAY	TUESDAY	WEDNESDAY
1	2	3	4
8	9	10	11
15	16	17	18
22	23	24	25
29	30	31	

OCTOBER

THURSDAY	FRIDAY	SATURDAY	NOTES/GOALS
5	6	7	
12	13	14	
19	20	21	
26	27	28	

WEEKLY FOOD DIARY

	MONDAY	TUESDAY	WEDNESDAY	THURSDAY	FRIDAY	SATURDAY	SUNDAY
BREAKFAST							
LUNCH							
DINNER							
SNACKS							
DAILY TOTALS	FRUIT ___ VEG ___ FAT ___ PROTEIN ___ BREAD ___ MILK ___ FLOATING ___	FRUIT ___ VEG ___ FAT ___ PROTEIN ___ BREAD ___ MILK ___ FLOATING ___	FRUIT ___ VEG ___ FAT ___ PROTEIN ___ BREAD ___ MILK ___ FLOATING ___	FRUIT ___ VEG ___ FAT ___ PROTEIN ___ BREAD ___ MILK ___ FLOATING ___	FRUIT ___ VEG ___ FAT ___ PROTEIN ___ BREAD ___ MILK ___ FLOATING ___	FRUIT ___ VEG ___ FAT ___ PROTEIN ___ BREAD ___ MILK ___ FLOATING ___	FRUIT ___ VEG ___ FAT ___ PROTEIN ___ BREAD ___ MILK ___ FLOATING ___

WEEKLY LIMITS   EGGS _____   CHEESE _____   MEAT _____   ORGAN MEAT _____   OPTIONAL CALORIES _____

I will attend my Weight Watchers meeting this week on _____

ENGAGEMENTS

OCTOBER

1 9 8 9

MONDAY

2

TUESDAY

3

WEDNESDAY

4

THURSDAY

5

FRIDAY

6

SATURDAY

7

SUNDAY

8

	S	M	T	W	T	F	S
						1	2
S	3	4	5	6	7	8	9
E	10	11	12	13	14	15	16
P	17	18	19	20	21	22	23
T	24	25	26	27	28	29	30

	S	M	T	W	T	F	S
	1	2	3	4	5	6	7
O	8	9	10	11	12	13	14
C	15	16	17	18	19	20	21
T	22	23	24	25	26	27	28
	29	30	31				

	S	M	T	W	T	F	S
			1	2	3	4	
N	5	6	7	8	9	10	11
O	12	13	14	15	16	17	18
V	19	20	21	22	23	24	25
	26	27	28	29	30		

WEEKLY FOOD DIARY

	MONDAY	TUESDAY	WEDNESDAY	THURSDAY	FRIDAY	SATURDAY	SUNDAY
BREAKFAST							
LUNCH							
DINNER							
SNACKS							
DAILY TOTALS	FRUIT ___ VEG ___ FAT ___ PROTEIN ___ BREAD ___ MILK ___ FLOATING ___	FRUIT ___ VEG ___ FAT ___ PROTEIN ___ BREAD ___ MILK ___ FLOATING ___	FRUIT ___ VEG ___ FAT ___ PROTEIN ___ BREAD ___ MILK ___ FLOATING ___	FRUIT ___ VEG ___ FAT ___ PROTEIN ___ BREAD ___ MILK ___ FLOATING ___	FRUIT ___ VEG ___ FAT ___ PROTEIN ___ BREAD ___ MILK ___ FLOATING ___	FRUIT ___ VEG ___ FAT ___ PROTEIN ___ BREAD ___ MILK ___ FLOATING ___	FRUIT ___ VEG ___ FAT ___ PROTEIN ___ BREAD ___ MILK ___ FLOATING ___

WEEKLY LIMITS   EGGS ___   CHEESE ___   MEAT ___   ORGAN MEAT ___   OPTIONAL CALORIES ___

I will attend my Weight Watchers meeting this week on ___

OCTOBER

Columbus Day (observed)
Yom Kippur
Thanksgiving Day (Canada)

MONDAY
9

TUESDAY
10

WEDNESDAY
11

Columbus Day

THURSDAY
12

FRIDAY
13

SATURDAY
14

SUNDAY
15

	S	M	T	W	T	F	S
						1	2
S	3	4	5	6	7	8	9
E	10	11	12	13	14	15	16
P	17	18	19	20	21	22	23
T	24	25	26	27	28	29	30

	S	M	T	W	T	F	S
	1	2	3	4	5	6	7
O	8	9	10	11	12	13	14
C	15	16	17	18	19	20	21
T	22	23	24	25	26	27	28
	29	30	31				

	S	M	T	W	T	F	S
				1	2	3	4
N	5	6	7	8	9	10	11
O	12	13	14	15	16	17	18
V	19	20	21	22	23	24	25
	26	27	28	29	30		

WEEKLY FOOD DIARY

	MONDAY	TUESDAY	WEDNESDAY	THURSDAY	FRIDAY	SATURDAY	SUNDAY
BREAKFAST							
LUNCH							
DINNER							
SNACKS							
DAILY TOTALS	FRUIT ___ VEG ___ FAT ___ PROTEIN ___ BREAD ___ MILK ___ FLOATING ___	FRUIT ___ VEG ___ FAT ___ PROTEIN ___ BREAD ___ MILK ___ FLOATING ___	FRUIT ___ VEG ___ FAT ___ PROTEIN ___ BREAD ___ MILK ___ FLOATING ___	FRUIT ___ VEG ___ FAT ___ PROTEIN ___ BREAD ___ MILK ___ FLOATING ___	FRUIT ___ VEG ___ FAT ___ PROTEIN ___ BREAD ___ MILK ___ FLOATING ___	FRUIT ___ VEG ___ FAT ___ PROTEIN ___ BREAD ___ MILK ___ FLOATING ___	FRUIT ___ VEG ___ FAT ___ PROTEIN ___ BREAD ___ MILK ___ FLOATING ___

WEEKLY LIMITS EGGS _____ CHEESE _____ MEAT _____ ORGAN MEAT _____ OPTIONAL CALORIES _____

I will attend my Weight Watchers meeting this week on _____

MONDAY
16

TUESDAY
17

WEDNESDAY
18

THURSDAY
19

FRIDAY
20

SATURDAY
21

SUNDAY
22

	S	M	T	W	T	F	S
SEPT						1	2
	3	4	5	6	7	8	9
	10	11	12	13	14	15	16
	17	18	19	20	21	22	23
	24	25	26	27	28	29	30

	S	M	T	W	T	F	S
	1	2	3	4	5	6	7
OCT	8	9	10	11	12	13	14
	15	16	17	18	19	20	21
	22	23	24	25	26	27	28
	29	30	31				

	S	M	T	W	T	F	S
				1	2	3	4
NOV	5	6	7	8	9	10	11
	12	13	14	15	16	17	18
	19	20	21	22	23	24	25
	26	27	28	29	30		

WEEKLY FOOD DIARY

	MONDAY	TUESDAY	WEDNESDAY	THURSDAY	FRIDAY	SATURDAY	SUNDAY
BREAKFAST							
LUNCH							
DINNER							
SNACKS							
DAILY TOTALS	FRUIT ___ VEG ___ FAT ___ PROTEIN ___ BREAD ___ MILK ___ FLOATING ___	FRUIT ___ VEG ___ FAT ___ PROTEIN ___ BREAD ___ MILK ___ FLOATING ___	FRUIT ___ VEG ___ FAT ___ PROTEIN ___ BREAD ___ MILK ___ FLOATING ___	FRUIT ___ VEG ___ FAT ___ PROTEIN ___ BREAD ___ MILK ___ FLOATING ___	FRUIT ___ VEG ___ FAT ___ PROTEIN ___ BREAD ___ MILK ___ FLOATING ___	FRUIT ___ VEG ___ FAT ___ PROTEIN ___ BREAD ___ MILK ___ FLOATING ___	FRUIT ___ VEG ___ FAT ___ PROTEIN ___ BREAD ___ MILK ___ FLOATING ___

WEEKLY LIMITS   EGGS _____   CHEESE _____   MEAT _____   ORGAN MEAT _____   OPTIONAL CALORIES _____

I will attend my Weight Watchers meeting this week on_____

MONDAY
23

United Nations Day

TUESDAY
24

WEDNESDAY
25

THURSDAY
26

FRIDAY
27

SATURDAY
28

SUNDAY
29

	S	M	T	W	T	F	S
S						1	2
E	3	4	5	6	7	8	9
P	10	11	12	13	14	15	16
T	17	18	19	20	21	22	23
	24	25	26	27	28	29	30

	S	M	T	W	T	F	S
	1	2	3	4	5	6	7
O	8	9	10	11	12	13	14
C	15	16	17	18	19	20	21
T	22	23	24	25	26	27	28
	29	30	31				

	S	M	T	W	T	F	S
				1	2	3	4
N	5	6	7	8	9	10	11
O	12	13	14	15	16	17	18
V	19	20	21	22	23	24	25
	26	27	28	29	30		

Smoked Salmon Crescents

Makes 4 servings, 2 crescents each

Refrigerated biscuits make this appetizer easy to prepare.

⅓ cup plus 2 teaspoons whipped cream cheese

2 ounces smoked salmon (lox), diced

2 tablespoons chopped scallion (green onion)

1 tablespoon chopped fresh dill

4 ready-to-bake refrigerated buttermilk flaky biscuits (1 ounce each unbaked)*

Preheat oven to 425°F. Using a fork, in small mixing bowl combine all ingredients except biscuits, mixing until thoroughly combined. Carefully separate each biscuit into 2 thin layers of dough and roll each between 2 sheets of wax paper, forming eight 5-inch circles. Spoon an equal amount of salmon mixture (about 2½ teaspoons) onto center of each layer of dough and fold each in half, turnover style; using the tines of a fork, press edges to seal. Using a sharp knife, gently cut through top of each crescent to allow steam to escape during baking. Transfer crescents to nonstick baking sheet and bake until puffed and lightly browned, 12 to 15 minutes.

Each serving provides: ½ Protein Exchange; 1 Bread Exchange; 50 Optional Calories

Per serving: 152 calories; 5 g protein; 9 g fat; 13 g carbohydrate; 18 mg calcium; 447 mg sodium; 19 mg cholesterol; 0.6 g dietary fiber

* Keep biscuits refrigerated until ready to use. Separate dough into layers as soon as biscuits are removed from the refrigerator; they will be difficult to work with if allowed to come to room temperature.

Pistachio-Popcorn Brittle

Makes 4 servings, about 1 cup each

For crunch when you munch, be sure to store this snack in an airtight container.

¼ cup firmly packed light brown sugar	1 tablespoon whipped butter
2 tablespoons light corn syrup	1 teaspoon vanilla extract
1 tablespoon plus 1 teaspoon margarine	4 cups plain prepared popcorn
	½ ounce chopped pistachio nuts

In 1-quart saucepan combine all ingredients except popcorn and nuts; cook over medium heat, stirring occasionally, until sugar is dissolved and mixture comes to a boil. Set candy thermometer in pan and continue cooking until temperature reaches 250°F or until a drop of mixture forms a hard yet pliable ball when dropped into cold water, 3 to 4 minutes. Remove pan from heat. In medium mixing bowl combine popcorn and nuts; add sugar mixture and stir until thoroughly combined. Let cool before serving.

Each serving provides: ½ Bread Exchange; 1 Fat Exchange; 130 Optional Calories

Per serving: 200 calories; 2 g protein; 10 g fat; 27 g carbohydrate; 25 mg calcium; 100 mg sodium; 12 mg cholesterol; 0 g dietary fiber*

* This figure does not include pistachio nuts; nutrition analysis not available.

WEIGHT

RECIPE

WATCHERS

Brown Rice Tabouleh

Makes 2 servings

Save time by using leftover rice in this flavorful salad.

1 cup cooked brown rice
4 ounces diced cooked chicken*
8 sun-dried tomato halves (not packed in oil), *or* 2 medium tomatoes, chopped
¼ cup *each* minced scallion (green onion), red bell pepper, fresh mint, and Italian (flat-leaf) parsley

2 tablespoons freshly squeezed lemon juice
1 tablespoon olive oil
1 small garlic clove, mashed
Dash *each* salt and pepper
Garnish: lemon slices and parsley sprigs

In medium salad bowl combine all ingredients except garnish. Cover with plastic wrap and refrigerate until ready to serve. Serve garnished with lemon and parsley.

Each serving provides: 2 Protein Exchanges; 1 Bread Exchange; 2½ Vegetable Exchanges; 1½ Fat Exchanges

Per serving with chicken and sun-dried tomatoes: 346 calories; 22 g protein; 12 g fat; 39 g carbohydrate; 63 mg calcium; 678 mg sodium (estimated); 50 mg cholesterol; 5 g dietary fiber

With chicken and fresh tomatoes: 346 calories; 22 g protein; 12 g fat; 39 g carbohydrate; 63 mg calcium; 138 mg sodium; 50 mg cholesterol; 5 g dietary fiber

* Turkey may be substituted for the chicken.

Per serving with turkey and sun-dried tomatoes: 333 calories; 22 g protein; 11 g fat; 39 g carbohydrate; 69 mg calcium; 672 mg sodium (estimated); 44 mg cholesterol; 5 g dietary fiber

With turkey and fresh tomatoes: 333 calories; 22 g protein; 11 g fat; 39 g carbohydrate; 69 mg calcium; 132 mg sodium; 44 mg cholesterol; 5 g dietary fiber

Pecan Cookies

Makes 24 servings, 2 cookies each

2¼ cups all-purpose flour
2 ounces finely ground pecans
1 teaspoon ground cinnamon
¼ teaspoon aniseed (optional)
1 cup granulated sugar

½ cup *each* whipped butter and
  margarine
1 egg
1 teaspoon vanilla extract

Preheat over to 350°F. In small mixing bowl combine flour, pecans, cinnamon, and, if desired, aniseed; set aside. Using electric mixer, in large mixing bowl beat together sugar, butter, margarine, egg, and vanilla until mixture is light and fluffy and double in volume. Gradually stir in flour mixture.

Onto nonstick cookie sheet drop dough by rounded tablespoonfuls, forming 24 cookies and leaving a space of about ¼ inch between each. Bake in middle of center oven rack until edges of cookies just turn golden, 8 to 10 minutes; using a spatula, remove cookies to wire rack to cool (cookies will harden as they cool). Repeat procedure making 24 more cookies.

Each serving provides: ½ Bread Exchange; 1 Fat Exchange; 80 Optional Calories

Per serving: 129 calories; 2 g protein; 6 g fat; 18 g carbohydrate; 6 mg calcium; 45 mg sodium; 17 mg cholesterol; 0.6 g dietary fiber

NOVEMBER

SUNDAY	MONDAY	TUESDAY	WEDNESDAY
			1
5	6	7	8
12	13	14	15
19	20	21	22
26	27	28	29

NOVEMBER

THURSDAY	FRIDAY	SATURDAY	NOTES/GOALS
2	3	4	
9	10	11	
16	17	18	
23	24	25	
30			

WEEKLY FOOD DIARY

	MONDAY	TUESDAY	WEDNESDAY	THURSDAY	FRIDAY	SATURDAY	SUNDAY
BREAKFAST							
LUNCH							
DINNER							
SNACKS							
DAILY TOTALS	FRUIT ___ VEG ___ FAT ___ PROTEIN ___ BREAD ___ MILK ___ FLOATING ___	FRUIT ___ VEG ___ FAT ___ PROTEIN ___ BREAD ___ MILK ___ FLOATING ___	FRUIT ___ VEG ___ FAT ___ PROTEIN ___ BREAD ___ MILK ___ FLOATING ___	FRUIT ___ VEG ___ FAT ___ PROTEIN ___ BREAD ___ MILK ___ FLOATING ___	FRUIT ___ VEG ___ FAT ___ PROTEIN ___ BREAD ___ MILK ___ FLOATING ___	FRUIT ___ VEG ___ FAT ___ PROTEIN ___ BREAD ___ MILK ___ FLOATING ___	FRUIT ___ VEG ___ FAT ___ PROTEIN ___ BREAD ___ MILK ___ FLOATING ___

WEEKLY LIMITS   EGGS _____   CHEESE _____   MEAT _____   ORGAN MEAT _____   OPTIONAL CALORIES _____

I will attend my Weight Watchers meeting this week on _____

MONDAY
30

Halloween

TUESDAY
31

WEDNESDAY
1

THURSDAY
2

FRIDAY
3

SATURDAY
4

SUNDAY
5

	S	M	T	W	T	F	S
		1	2	3	4	5	6	7
O	8	9	10	11	12	13	14
C	15	16	17	18	19	20	21
T	22	23	24	25	26	27	28
	29	30	31				

	S	M	T	W	T	F	S
				1	2	3	4
N	5	6	7	8	9	10	11
O	12	13	14	15	16	17	18
V	19	20	21	22	23	24	25
	26	27	28	29	30		

	S	M	T	W	T	F	S
						1	2
D	3	4	5	6	7	8	9
E	10	11	12	13	14	15	16
C	17	18	19	20	21	22	23
	24	25	26	27	28	29	30
	31						

WEEKLY FOOD DIARY

	MONDAY	TUESDAY	WEDNESDAY	THURSDAY	FRIDAY	SATURDAY	SUNDAY
BREAKFAST							
LUNCH							
DINNER							
SNACKS							
DAILY TOTALS	FRUIT ____ VEG ____ FAT ____ PROTEIN ____ BREAD ____ MILK ____ FLOATING ____	FRUIT ____ VEG ____ FAT ____ PROTEIN ____ BREAD ____ MILK ____ FLOATING ____	FRUIT ____ VEG ____ FAT ____ PROTEIN ____ BREAD ____ MILK ____ FLOATING ____	FRUIT ____ VEG ____ FAT ____ PROTEIN ____ BREAD ____ MILK ____ FLOATING ____	FRUIT ____ VEG ____ FAT ____ PROTEIN ____ BREAD ____ MILK ____ FLOATING ____	FRUIT ____ VEG ____ FAT ____ PROTEIN ____ BREAD ____ MILK ____ FLOATING ____	FRUIT ____ VEG ____ FAT ____ PROTEIN ____ BREAD ____ MILK ____ FLOATING ____

WEEKLY LIMITS   EGGS ____   CHEESE ____   MEAT ____   ORGAN MEAT ____   OPTIONAL CALORIES ____

I will attend my Weight Watchers meeting this week on ____

MONDAY
6

Election Day

TUESDAY
7

WEDNESDAY
8

THURSDAY
9

FRIDAY
10

Veterans Day
Armistice Day (Canada)

SATURDAY
11

SUNDAY
12

	S	M	T	W	T	F	S
		1	2	3	4	5	6	7
O	8	9	10	11	12	13	14
C	15	16	17	18	19	20	21
T	22	23	24	25	26	27	28
	29	30	31				

	S	M	T	W	T	F	S
				1	2	3	4
N	5	6	7	8	9	10	11
O	12	13	14	15	16	17	18
V	19	20	21	22	23	24	25
	26	27	28	29	30		

	S	M	T	W	T	F	S
						1	2
D	3	4	5	6	7	8	9
E	10	11	12	13	14	15	16
C	17	18	19	20	21	22	23
	24	25	26	27	28	29	30
	31						

WEEKLY FOOD DIARY

	MONDAY	TUESDAY	WEDNESDAY	THURSDAY	FRIDAY	SATURDAY	SUNDAY
BREAKFAST							
LUNCH							
DINNER							
SNACKS							
DAILY TOTALS	FRUIT ___ VEG ___ FAT ___ PROTEIN ___ BREAD ___ MILK ___ FLOATING ___	FRUIT ___ VEG ___ FAT ___ PROTEIN ___ BREAD ___ MILK ___ FLOATING ___	FRUIT ___ VEG ___ FAT ___ PROTEIN ___ BREAD ___ MILK ___ FLOATING ___	FRUIT ___ VEG ___ FAT ___ PROTEIN ___ BREAD ___ MILK ___ FLOATING ___	FRUIT ___ VEG ___ FAT ___ PROTEIN ___ BREAD ___ MILK ___ FLOATING ___	FRUIT ___ VEG ___ FAT ___ PROTEIN ___ BREAD ___ MILK ___ FLOATING ___	FRUIT ___ VEG ___ FAT ___ PROTEIN ___ BREAD ___ MILK ___ FLOATING ___

WEEKLY LIMITS   EGGS _____   CHEESE _____   MEAT _____   ORGAN MEAT _____   OPTIONAL CALORIES _____

I will attend my Weight Watchers meeting this week on _____

ENGAGEMENTS

NOVEMBER

1 9 8 9

MONDAY
13

TUESDAY
14

WEDNESDAY
15

THURSDAY
16

FRIDAY
17

SATURDAY
18

SUNDAY
19

	S	M	T	W	T	F	S
		1	2	3	4	5	6	7
O	8	9	10	11	12	13	14
C	15	16	17	18	19	20	21
T	22	23	24	25	26	27	28
	29	30	31				

	S	M	T	W	T	F	S
				1	2	3	4
N	5	6	7	8	9	10	11
O	12	13	14	15	16	17	18
V	19	20	21	22	23	24	25
	26	27	28	29	30		

	S	M	T	W	T	F	S
						1	2
D	3	4	5	6	7	8	9
E	10	11	12	13	14	15	16
C	17	18	19	20	21	22	23
	24	25	26	27	28	29	30
	31						

WEEKLY FOOD DIARY

	MONDAY	TUESDAY	WEDNESDAY	THURSDAY	FRIDAY	SATURDAY	SUNDAY
BREAKFAST							
LUNCH							
DINNER							
SNACKS							
DAILY TOTALS	FRUIT ___ VEG ___ FAT ___ PROTEIN ___ BREAD ___ MILK ___ FLOATING ___	FRUIT ___ VEG ___ FAT ___ PROTEIN ___ BREAD ___ MILK ___ FLOATING ___	FRUIT ___ VEG ___ FAT ___ PROTEIN ___ BREAD ___ MILK ___ FLOATING ___	FRUIT ___ VEG ___ FAT ___ PROTEIN ___ BREAD ___ MILK ___ FLOATING ___	FRUIT ___ VEG ___ FAT ___ PROTEIN ___ BREAD ___ MILK ___ FLOATING ___	FRUIT ___ VEG ___ FAT ___ PROTEIN ___ BREAD ___ MILK ___ FLOATING ___	FRUIT ___ VEG ___ FAT ___ PROTEIN ___ BREAD ___ MILK ___ FLOATING ___

WEEKLY LIMITS EGGS _____ CHEESE _____ MEAT _____ ORGAN MEAT _____ OPTIONAL CALORIES _____

I will attend my Weight Watchers meeting this week on _____

NOVEMBER

1 9 8 9

MONDAY
20

TUESDAY
21

WEDNESDAY
22

Thanksgiving Day

THURSDAY
23

FRIDAY
24

SATURDAY
25

SUNDAY
26

	S	M	T	W	T	F	S
	1	2	3	4	5	6	7
O	8	9	10	11	12	13	14
C	15	16	17	18	19	20	21
T	22	23	24	25	26	27	28
	29	30	31				

	S	M	T	W	T	F	S
				1	2	3	4
N	5	6	7	8	9	10	11
O	12	13	14	15	16	17	18
V	19	20	21	22	23	24	25
	26	27	28	29	30		

	S	M	T	W	T	F	S
						1	2
D	3	4	5	6	7	8	9
E	10	11	12	13	14	15	16
C	17	18	19	20	21	22	23
	24	25	26	27	28	29	30
	31						

WEEKLY FOOD DIARY

	MONDAY	TUESDAY	WEDNESDAY	THURSDAY	FRIDAY	SATURDAY	SUNDAY
BREAKFAST							
LUNCH							
DINNER							
SNACKS							
DAILY TOTALS	FRUIT ___ VEG ___ FAT ___ PROTEIN ___ BREAD ___ MILK ___ FLOATING ___	FRUIT ___ VEG ___ FAT ___ PROTEIN ___ BREAD ___ MILK ___ FLOATING ___	FRUIT ___ VEG ___ FAT ___ PROTEIN ___ BREAD ___ MILK ___ FLOATING ___	FRUIT ___ VEG ___ FAT ___ PROTEIN ___ BREAD ___ MILK ___ FLOATING ___	FRUIT ___ VEG ___ FAT ___ PROTEIN ___ BREAD ___ MILK ___ FLOATING ___	FRUIT ___ VEG ___ FAT ___ PROTEIN ___ BREAD ___ MILK ___ FLOATING ___	FRUIT ___ VEG ___ FAT ___ PROTEIN ___ BREAD ___ MILK ___ FLOATING ___

WEEKLY LIMITS   EGGS ___   CHEESE ___   MEAT ___   ORGAN MEAT ___   OPTIONAL CALORIES ___

I will attend my Weight Watchers meeting this week on ___

MONDAY
27

TUESDAY
28

WEDNESDAY
29

THURSDAY
30

FRIDAY
1

SATURDAY
2

SUNDAY
3

	S	M	T	W	T	F	S
		1	2	3	4	5	6	7
O	8	9	10	11	12	13	14
C	15	16	17	18	19	20	21
T	22	23	24	25	26	27	28
	29	30	31				

	S	M	T	W	T	F	S
				1	2	3	4
N	5	6	7	8	9	10	11
O	12	13	14	15	16	17	18
V	19	20	21	22	23	24	25
	26	27	28	29	30		

	S	M	T	W	T	F	S
						1	2
D	3	4	5	6	7	8	9
E	10	11	12	13	14	15	16
C	17	18	19	20	21	22	23
	24	25	26	27	28	29	30
	31						

Turkey Cutlets with Gingersnap Sauce

Makes 2 servings

1 tablespoon olive *or* vegetable oil
2 thin-sliced turkey cutlets (3 ounces each)
¼ cup chopped onion
¾ cup canned ready-to-serve chicken broth

1 tablespoon red wine vinegar
3 gingersnap cookies (½ ounce), made into crumbs
3 tablespoons sour cream
¼ teaspoon caraway seed
Dash white pepper

In 10-inch nonstick skillet heat oil; add turkey and cook over medium-high heat, turning once, until lightly browned on both sides and cooked through, 1 to 2 minutes on each side. Remove from skillet and set aside.

To same skillet add onion and sauté until softened, about 1 minute; add broth and vinegar and bring to a boil. Stir in gingersnap crumbs and, continuing to stir, cook until crumbs are moistened and mixture thickens. Stir in sour cream, caraway seed, and pepper.

Reduce heat to low and let cook until flavors blend, 2 to 3 minutes. Return turkey to skillet and cook until turkey is heated through, about 1 minute longer.

Each serving provides: 2 Protein Exchanges; ¼ Vegetable Exchange; 1½ Fat Exchanges; 105 Optional Calories

Per serving: 254 calories; 22 g protein; 14 g fat; 9 g carbohydrate; 47 mg calcium; 486 mg sodium; 65 mg cholesterol; 0.2 g dietary fiber*

* This figure does not include gingersnaps; nutrition analysis not available.

Layered Mexican Dip

Makes 4 servings

2 teaspoons olive *or* vegetable oil
2 tablespoons *each* chopped onion and green bell pepper
1 garlic clove, minced
6 ounces drained canned pinto *or* red kidney beans, slightly mashed
2 teaspoons *each* chopped fresh cilantro (Chinese parsley) *or* Italian (flat-leaf) parsley and chili powder

¼ cup *each* sour cream and diced tomato
1 ounce Cheddar *or* Colby cheese, shredded
¼ avocado (2 ounces), pared and diced
4 pitted black olives, sliced
4 corn tortillas (6-inch diameter each), lightly toasted and each cut into 6 equal wedges

In 8-inch nonstick skillet heat oil; add onion, bell pepper, and garlic and sauté over medium-high heat, stirring frequently, until vegetables are softened, 1 to 2 minutes. Add beans and seasonings, and cook, stirring frequently, until mixture is heated through, 2 to 3 minutes.

Over bottom of 2-cup casserole spread bean mixture in an even layer; spread sour cream evenly over bean mixture. Top with tomato, then sprinkle with cheese, avocado, and olives. Serve with tortilla wedges for dipping.

Each serving provides: 1 Protein Exchange; 1 Bread Exchange; ¼ Vegetable Exchange; ½ Fat Exchange; 65 Optional Calories

Per serving with pinto beans: 239 calories; 9 g protein; 12 g fat; 27 g carbohydrate; 144 mg calcium; 292 mg sodium; 14 mg cholesterol; 5 g dietary fiber

With kidney beans: 237 calories; 8 g protein; 12 g fat; 26 g carbohydrate; 138 mg calcium; 291 mg sodium; 13 mg cholesterol; 2 g dietary fiber

WEIGHT

RECIPE

WATCHERS

"Reuben" Muffins

Makes 6 servings, 2 muffins each

These muffins freeze well so they can be prepared in advance and kept for future use. Then just reheat for a fast and delicious light meal.

6 ounces skinned and boned cooked turkey, minced

1 cup rinsed and drained sauerkraut, chopped*

3 ounces Swiss *or* Jarlsberg cheese, shredded

3 eggs, beaten

3 tablespoons Thousand Island dressing

½ teaspoon double-acting baking powder

Preheat oven to 400°F. Line twelve 2½-inch-diameter muffin pan cups with paper baking cups; set aside. In large mixing bowl combine all ingredients until blended. Fill each baking cup with an equal amount of turkey mixture (each will be about ⅔ full). Bake until muffins are slightly puffed and golden brown, about 20 minutes. Serve warm or at room temperature.

Each serving provides: 2 Protein Exchanges; ¼ Vegetable Exchange; 1 Fat Exchange

Per serving: 174 calories; 16 g protein; 11 g fat; 3 g carbohydrate; 183 mg calcium; 273 mg sodium; 172 mg cholesterol; 0.5 g dietary fiber

* Use the sauerkraut that is packaged in plastic bags and stored in the refrigerator section of the supermarket; it is usually crisper and less salty than the canned.

Herbed Apple Sorbet

Makes 4 servings, about ⅓ cup each

3 tablespoons freshly squeezed lemon juice
1 tablespoon granulated sugar
½ teaspoon minced fresh rosemary *or* mint

1 pound Golden Delicious apples, cored, pared, and sliced
Garnish: rosemary *or* mint sprigs

In 1-quart saucepan combine juice and sugar and cook over medium heat, stirring constantly, until sugar is dissolved. Stir in minced rosemary (or mint); set aside. In work bowl of food processor fitted with steel blade, process apples until pureed. Add puree to lemon juice mixture; return saucepan to medium heat and cook, stirring frequently, until heated, about 2 minutes. Transfer mixture to a shallow freezer-safe bowl; cover with plastic wrap and freeze until mixture is just firm, 1 to 2 hours. To serve, spoon into 4 dessert dishes and garnish with rosemary (or mint) sprigs.

Each serving provides: 1 Fruit Exchange; 15 Optional Calories
Per serving: 70 calories; 0.2 g protein; 0.3 g fat; 18 g carbohydrate; 5 mg calcium; 0.2 mg sodium; 0 mg cholesterol; 2 g dietary fiber

DECEMBER

SUNDAY	MONDAY	TUESDAY	WEDNESDAY
3	4	5	6
10	11	12	13
17	18	19	20
24 / 31	25	26	27

DECEMBER

THURSDAY	FRIDAY	SATURDAY	NOTES/GOALS
	1	2	
7	8	9	
14	15	16	
21	22	23	
28	29	30	

WEEKLY FOOD DIARY

	MONDAY	TUESDAY	WEDNESDAY	THURSDAY	FRIDAY	SATURDAY	SUNDAY
BREAKFAST							
LUNCH							
DINNER							
SNACKS							
DAILY TOTALS	FRUIT ___ VEG ___ FAT ___ PROTEIN ___ BREAD ___ MILK ___ FLOATING ___	FRUIT ___ VEG ___ FAT ___ PROTEIN ___ BREAD ___ MILK ___ FLOATING ___	FRUIT ___ VEG ___ FAT ___ PROTEIN ___ BREAD ___ MILK ___ FLOATING ___	FRUIT ___ VEG ___ FAT ___ PROTEIN ___ BREAD ___ MILK ___ FLOATING ___	FRUIT ___ VEG ___ FAT ___ PROTEIN ___ BREAD ___ MILK ___ FLOATING ___	FRUIT ___ VEG ___ FAT ___ PROTEIN ___ BREAD ___ MILK ___ FLOATING ___	FRUIT ___ VEG ___ FAT ___ PROTEIN ___ BREAD ___ MILK ___ FLOATING ___

WEEKLY LIMITS   EGGS ___   CHEESE ___   MEAT ___   ORGAN MEAT ___   OPTIONAL CALORIES ___

I will attend my Weight Watchers meeting this week on _____

MONDAY

4

TUESDAY

5

WEDNESDAY

6

THURSDAY

7

FRIDAY

8

SATURDAY

9

SUNDAY

10

	S	M	T	W	T	F	S
					1	2	3	4
N	5	6	7	8	9	10	11
O	12	13	14	15	16	17	18
V	19	20	21	22	23	24	25
	26	27	28	29	30		

	S	M	T	W	T	F	S
						1	2
D	3	4	5	6	7	8	9
E	10	11	12	13	14	15	16
C	17	18	19	20	21	22	23
	24	25	26	27	28	29	30
	31						

	S	M	T	W	T	F	S
		1	2	3	4	5	6
J	7	8	9	10	11	12	13
A	14	15	16	17	18	19	20
N	21	22	23	24	25	26	27
	28	29	30	31			

WEEKLY FOOD DIARY

	MONDAY	TUESDAY	WEDNESDAY	THURSDAY	FRIDAY	SATURDAY	SUNDAY
BREAKFAST							
LUNCH							
DINNER							
SNACKS							
DAILY TOTALS	FRUIT ___ VEG ___ FAT ___ PROTEIN ___ BREAD ___ MILK ___ FLOATING ___	FRUIT ___ VEG ___ FAT ___ PROTEIN ___ BREAD ___ MILK ___ FLOATING ___	FRUIT ___ VEG ___ FAT ___ PROTEIN ___ BREAD ___ MILK ___ FLOATING ___	FRUIT ___ VEG ___ FAT ___ PROTEIN ___ BREAD ___ MILK ___ FLOATING ___	FRUIT ___ VEG ___ FAT ___ PROTEIN ___ BREAD ___ MILK ___ FLOATING ___	FRUIT ___ VEG ___ FAT ___ PROTEIN ___ BREAD ___ MILK ___ FLOATING ___	FRUIT ___ VEG ___ FAT ___ PROTEIN ___ BREAD ___ MILK ___ FLOATING ___

WEEKLY LIMITS EGGS _____ CHEESE _____ MEAT _____ ORGAN MEAT _____ OPTIONAL CALORIES _____

I will attend my Weight Watchers meeting this week on _____

MONDAY
11

TUESDAY
12

WEDNESDAY
13

THURSDAY
14

FRIDAY
15

SATURDAY
16

SUNDAY
17

	S	M	T	W	T	F	S
				1	2	3	4
N	5	6	7	8	9	10	11
O	12	13	14	15	16	17	18
V	19	20	21	22	23	24	25
	26	27	28	29	30		

	S	M	T	W	T	F	S
						1	2
D	3	4	5	6	7	8	9
E	10	11	12	13	14	15	16
C	17	18	19	20	21	22	23
	24	25	26	27	28	29	30
	31						

	S	M	T	W	T	F	S
		1	2	3	4	5	6
J	7	8	9	10	11	12	13
A	14	15	16	17	18	19	20
N	21	22	23	24	25	26	27
	28	29	30	31			

WEEKLY FOOD DIARY

	MONDAY	TUESDAY	WEDNESDAY	THURSDAY	FRIDAY	SATURDAY	SUNDAY
BREAKFAST							
LUNCH							
DINNER							
SNACKS							
DAILY TOTALS	FRUIT ___ VEG ___ FAT ___ PROTEIN ___ BREAD ___ MILK ___ FLOATING ___	FRUIT ___ VEG ___ FAT ___ PROTEIN ___ BREAD ___ MILK ___ FLOATING ___	FRUIT ___ VEG ___ FAT ___ PROTEIN ___ BREAD ___ MILK ___ FLOATING ___	FRUIT ___ VEG ___ FAT ___ PROTEIN ___ BREAD ___ MILK ___ FLOATING ___	FRUIT ___ VEG ___ FAT ___ PROTEIN ___ BREAD ___ MILK ___ FLOATING ___	FRUIT ___ VEG ___ FAT ___ PROTEIN ___ BREAD ___ MILK ___ FLOATING ___	FRUIT ___ VEG ___ FAT ___ PROTEIN ___ BREAD ___ MILK ___ FLOATING ___

WEEKLY LIMITS EGGS _____ CHEESE _____ MEAT _____ ORGAN MEAT _____ OPTIONAL CALORIES _____

I will attend my Weight Watchers meeting this week on _____

MONDAY
18

TUESDAY
19

WEDNESDAY
20

THURSDAY
21

FRIDAY
22

First Day of Hanukkah

SATURDAY
23

SUNDAY
24

	S	M	T	W	T	F	S
						1	2	3	4
N	5	6	7	8	9	10	11
O	12	13	14	15	16	17	18
V	19	20	21	22	23	24	25
	26	27	28	29	30		

	S	M	T	W	T	F	S
							1	2
	3	4	5	6	7	8	9
D	10	11	12	13	14	15	16
E	17	18	19	20	21	22	23
C	24	25	26	27	28	29	30
	31						

	S	M	T	W	T	F	S
		1	2	3	4	5	6
J	7	8	9	10	11	12	13
A	14	15	16	17	18	19	20
N	21	22	23	24	25	26	27
	28	29	30	31			

WEEKLY FOOD DIARY

	MONDAY	TUESDAY	WEDNESDAY	THURSDAY	FRIDAY	SATURDAY	SUNDAY
BREAKFAST							
LUNCH							
DINNER							
SNACKS							
DAILY TOTALS	FRUIT ___ VEG ___ FAT ___ PROTEIN ___ BREAD ___ MILK ___ FLOATING ___	FRUIT ___ VEG ___ FAT ___ PROTEIN ___ BREAD ___ MILK ___ FLOATING ___	FRUIT ___ VEG ___ FAT ___ PROTEIN ___ BREAD ___ MILK ___ FLOATING ___	FRUIT ___ VEG ___ FAT ___ PROTEIN ___ BREAD ___ MILK ___ FLOATING ___	FRUIT ___ VEG ___ FAT ___ PROTEIN ___ BREAD ___ MILK ___ FLOATING ___	FRUIT ___ VEG ___ FAT ___ PROTEIN ___ BREAD ___ MILK ___ FLOATING ___	FRUIT ___ VEG ___ FAT ___ PROTEIN ___ BREAD ___ MILK ___ FLOATING ___

WEEKLY LIMITS   EGGS _____   CHEESE _____   MEAT _____   ORGAN MEAT _____   OPTIONAL CALORIES _____

I will attend my Weight Watchers meeting this week on _____

ENGAGEMENTS

DECEMBER

1 9 8 9

Christmas Day

MONDAY
25

Boxing Day (Canada)

TUESDAY
26

WEDNESDAY
27

THURSDAY
28

FRIDAY
29

SATURDAY
30

New Year's Eve 1989

SUNDAY
31

	S	M	T	W	T	F	S
				1	2	3	4
N	5	6	7	8	9	10	11
O	12	13	14	15	16	17	18
V	19	20	21	22	23	24	25
	26	27	28	29	30		

	S	M	T	W	T	F	S
						1	2
	3	4	5	6	7	8	9
D	10	11	12	13	14	15	16
E	17	18	19	20	21	22	23
C	24	25	26	27	28	29	30
	31						

	S	M	T	W	T	F	S
		1	2	3	4	5	6
J	7	8	9	10	11	12	13
A	14	15	16	17	18	19	20
N	21	22	23	24	25	26	27
	28	29	30	31			

Pistachio Cheese Ball

Makes 8 servings

This elegant hors d'oeuvre may be made with any kind of blue cheese, although Gorgonzola is especially good. Prepare it up to 1 hour in advance and serve with crackers, celery sticks, or cucumber slices.

7 ounces Gorgonzola cheese (at room temperature)
3 tablespoons whipped cream cheese
1 ounce grated Parmesan cheese

2 tablespoons chopped fresh Italian (flat-leaf) parsley
1 tablespoon minced onion
1 ounce finely ground pistachio nuts

Using a fork, in small bowl mash cheeses together; add parsley and onion and stir to combine. Shape cheese mixture into a ball; wrap in plastic wrap and refrigerate until firm, about 30 minutes.

On sheet of wax paper or a paper plate spread nuts. Roll cheese ball in nuts until ball is thoroughly coated. Transfer to serving platter. Serve immediately or cover and refrigerate until ready to serve.

Each serving provides: 1 Protein Exchange; 40 Optional Calories

Per serving: 137 calories; 8 g protein; 11 g fat; 2 g carbohydrate; 189 mg calcium; 423 mg sodium; 25 mg cholesterol; trace dietary fiber*

* This figure does not include pistachio nuts; nutrition analysis not available.

WEIGHT RECIPE WATCHERS

Tomato Boats

Makes 2 servings, 2 "boats" each

Tired of serving the same old salad? Try this for a change of pace.

⅓ cup cottage cheese
1 tablespoon *each* minced carrot,
chives, and green bell pepper

Dash white pepper
2 large plum tomatoes
Garnish: parsley sprigs

In small bowl combine all ingredients except tomatoes and garnish; set aside. Cut each tomato in half lengthwise and scoop out and discard pulp and seeds, leaving a ¼-inch-thick shell. Fill each tomato shell with ¼ of the cheese mixture and garnish with parsley.

Each serving provides: ½ Protein Exchange; ½ Vegetable Exchange

Per serving: 49 calories; 5 g protein; 2 g fat; 4 g carbohydrate; 27 mg calcium; 146 mg sodium; 5 mg cholesterol; 0.6 g dietary fiber

Mexican Shrimp Broil

Makes 2 servings, 2 skewers each

Cilantro gives this dish a traditional Mexican flavor. Substitute Italian (flat-leaf) parsley and you transform it into an Italian scampi.

8 large shrimp (16–20s)*
1 tablespoon *each* chopped cilantro (Chinese parsley), olive oil, and freshly squeezed lime juice

½ small garlic clove, mashed
Dash *each* salt and pepper

Shell and devein shrimp, leaving last segment and tail in place. Onto each of four 10-inch wooden or metal skewers, starting at tail end, thread 2 shrimp lengthwise; transfer skewers to baking sheet; set aside.

Preheat broiler. In small bowl combine remaining ingredients and, using half of mixture, brush an equal amount over each shrimp. Broil until shrimp are golden, about 3 minutes. Turn shrimp over and brush with remaining oil mixture; broil until shrimp are firm, about 3 minutes longer (*do not overcook or shrimp will toughen*). Transfer to serving platter and pour any pan juice over shrimp.

Each serving provides: 2 Protein Exchanges; 1½ Fat Exchanges

Per serving: 138 calories; 14 g protein; 8 g fat; 2 g carbohydrate; 42 mg calcium; 172 mg sodium; 108 mg cholesterol; 0.1 g dietary fiber

* This indicates the approximate number of shrimp per pound before cooking, shelling, and deveining. Eight shrimp will yield about 4 ounces cooked seafood.

Green Chili Dip

Makes 4 servings, about 2 tablespoons each

This spicy dip can be prepared in advance. Store in resealable plastic container in refrigerator for up to 1 week. Serve as a snack with assorted fresh vegetables or as a topping on a baked potato.

⅓ cup plus 2 teaspoons sour cream
1 tablespoon *each* chopped scallion
   (green onion) and fresh *or* drained
   canned mild green chili pepper
1½ teaspoons chopped cilantro
   (Chinese parsley) *or* Italian (flat-leaf)
   parsley

½ small garlic clove, mashed
⅛ teaspoon salt
Dash ground red pepper

In small mixing bowl combine all ingredients until blended. Serve immediately or cover and refrigerate until ready to serve. Serve at room temperature.

Each serving provides: 50 Optional Calories

Per serving with fresh green chili pepper: 48 calories; 0.8 g protein; 5 g fat; 1 g carbohydrate; 28 mg calcium; 81 mg sodium; 9 mg cholesterol; 0.1 g dietary fiber

With canned green chili pepper: 48 calories; 0.8 g protein; 5 g fat; 1 g carbohydrate; 28 mg calcium; 94 mg sodium; 9 mg cholesterol; 0.1 g dietary fiber

Toast the new year and the new decade with a festive buffet for 10, served up in slenderizing style. Your guests will love our array of party dishes: Mushrooms with Crabmeat Stuffing, Italian Vegetable Tart, and bubbly Cherry-Berry Punch. If you like, add your own platter of assorted sliced meats or fruit and cheeses and a basket of rolls to round out the meal. And what's a party without dessert? Our Raspberry-Chocolate Loaf is so easy to make and it's simply divine!

Mushrooms with Crabmeat Stuffing

Makes 10 servings, 2 mushrooms each

Serve these tasty mushrooms hot from the oven or at room temperature.

3 tablespoons plus 1 teaspoon margarine
½ cup chopped scallions (green onions)
1 garlic clove, minced
10 ounces well-drained thawed frozen crabmeat
¼ cup dry sherry
3 tablespoons lemon juice

1 cup less 1 tablespoon plain dried bread crumbs
½ cup sour cream
Dash pepper
20 large mushroom caps
1 tablespoon plus 1 teaspoon grated Parmesan cheese

Preheat oven to 450°F. In 12-inch nonstick skillet melt margarine; add scallions and garlic and sauté over medium-high heat until softened, about 1 minute. Add crabmeat, sherry, and lemon juice and cook, stirring occasionally, until crabmeat is heated through, 2 to 3 minutes. Transfer to medium mixing bowl; stir in bread crumbs, sour cream, and pepper and mix well until thoroughly combined.

Fill each mushroom cap with an equal amount of crabmeat mixture (about 2 tablespoonfuls) and arrange on nonstick baking sheet; sprinkle stuffing with Parmesan cheese. Bake until stuffing is lightly browned and mushrooms are fork-tender, 12 to 15 minutes.

Each serving provides: 1 Protein Exchange; ½ Bread Exchange; 1 Vegetable Exchange; 1 Fat Exchange; 40 Optional Calories

Per serving: 150 calories; 9 g protein; 8 g fat; 11 g carbohydrate; 72 mg calcium; 215 mg sodium; 34 mg cholesterol; 1 g dietary fiber

Italian Vegetable Tart

Makes 10 servings

Red and yellow bell peppers add beautiful color and a delicious sweetness to this dish, but green peppers can be substituted.

1 refrigerated all-ready pizza crust dough (10 ounces)
1 tablespoon plus 2 teaspoons olive oil
1 cup *each* **thawed frozen artichoke hearts, cut into halves, julienne-cut leeks (white portion with some green), julienne-cut red bell peppers, julienne-cut yellow bell peppers, and diced tomatoes**

2 garlic cloves, minced
2 tablespoons chopped fresh basil *or* **1 teaspoon dried**
¼ pound Fontina cheese, shredded
1 ounce grated Parmesan cheese

Preheat oven to 425°F. Using rolling pin roll dough into a circle and then, using fingers, stretch into a 13-inch-diameter circle. Into 12-inch nonstick pizza pan, press dough into pan and fold under any dough that extends. Cover dough with sheet of foil and top with uncooked dry beans.* Bake until dough is cooked through and edges are lightly browned, about 10 minutes.

In 12-inch nonstick skillet heat oil; add vegetables and garlic and sauté over high heat, stirring frequently, until vegetables are tender-crisp, 2 to 3 minutes. Stir in basil and set aside.

Remove beans and foil from crust. Spread vegetable mixture evenly over crust to within ½ inch from edge; sprinkle Fontina cheese evenly over vegetables and top with Parmesan cheese. Broil until cheese is melted and lightly browned, 2 to 3 minutes. To serve, cut into 10 equal wedges.

Each serving provides: ½ Protein Exchange; 1 Bread Exchange; 1 Vegetable Exchange; ½ Fat Exchange

Per serving: 172 calories; 7 g protein; 8 g fat; 18 g carbohydrate; 119 mg calcium; 201 mg sodium; 15 mg cholesterol; 2 g dietary fiber

* Filling the unbaked pizza crust with dry beans will prevent bubbling during baking; save the beans as they can be used over and over again for this purpose.

Cherry-Berry Punch

Makes 10 servings, about 1 cup each

**1 quart plus 1 cup strawberries (reserve
10 for garnish)**
1 tablespoon granulated sugar
**1 quart plus 1 cup orange-flavored
seltzer, chilled***

½ cup cherry liqueur
Garnish: 10 lime *or* lemon slices

In blender container or work bowl of food processor fitted with steel blade combine all except reserved strawberries and the sugar and process until pureed, scraping down sides of container as necessary. Pour into punch bowl; stir in seltzer and liqueur. Serve each portion of punch with 1 reserved strawberry and 1 lime or lemon slice.

Each serving provides: ½ Fruit Exchange; 45 Optional Calories

Per serving: 61 calories; 0.5 g protein; 0.3 g fat; 10 g carbohydrate; 11 mg calcium; 0.8 g sodium; 0 mg cholesterol; 1 g dietary fiber

* If orange-flavored seltzer is not available, substitute regular seltzer and add 1 teaspoon grated orange rind.

Raspberry-Chocolate Loaf

Makes 10 servings, 1 slice each

This is a great way to dress up a frozen pound cake, or one from your local bakery, or a favorite recipe.

1 frozen pound cake loaf (10¾ ounces) slightly thawed
⅓ cup reduced-calorie raspberry spread (16 calories per 2 teaspoons), melted

4 ounces semisweet chocolate chips
⅓ cup whipped butter

Using a serrated knife, cut pound cake horizontally into 3 equal layers. Spread 2 tablespoons plus 2 teaspoons raspberry spread over cut side of bottom layer of pound cake; top with second pound-cake layer and spread with remaining raspberry spread. Set third cake layer cut-side down over preserves.

In double boiler combine chocolate and butter and cook over hot (*not boiling*) water, stirring frequently, until chocolate is melted and mixture is smooth.*

Place sheet of wax paper under a wire rack; set cake on rack. Spread chocolate mixture over top and sides of cake; scrape up any chocolate mixture that drips onto wax paper and spread over cake. Transfer cake to serving platter, cover loosely with plastic wrap, and refrigerate until chocolate hardens, about 5 minutes. To serve, cut into 10 equal slices.

Each serving provides: 235 Optional Calories

Per serving: 222 calories; 2 g protein; 14 g fat; 24 g carbohydrate; 15 mg calcium; 135 mg sodium; 8 mg cholesterol; 0 g dietary fiber

* When melting chocolate, it should not come in contact with water or steam; moisture will cause it to harden.

MEALS AWAY FROM HOME

Not very long ago, when families ate all their meals together and hot home-cooked breakfasts and dinners were the norm, eating away from home was usually reserved for special occasions. All that has changed as busy people everywhere juggle work, school, family, and social responsibilities. More responsibilities mean fewer home-cooked meals, and for those following a weight-loss program, more potential problems. You can avoid the problems if you plan ahead—and that's just what this section will help you do. Look over and use our ideas for nutritious take-along breakfasts, tasty brown-bag lunches, and creative coffee-break snacks.

Take-Along Breakfasts

You're running late again . . . there goes breakfast. Don't skip that all-important morning meal—take it with you!

1 small orange
¾ ounce cold cereal with ½ cup plain low-fat yogurt
Coffee or tea

½ medium banana
1 ounce sliced Swiss cheese
½ small bagel (1 ounce)
Coffee or tea

½ medium grapefruit
1 hard-cooked egg
1 slice whole wheat bread
Coffee or tea

1 medium peach
1 tablespoon peanut butter spread on 2 graham crackers (2½-inch squares)
Coffee or tea

Coffee Breaks

Pass up the donut- and Danish-laden coffee cart and bring your own special snack. Here are some break-time snacks that are easy and delicious—and they may even save you money.

- 1 serving reduced-calorie hot cocoa *or* flavored milk beverage
- a piece of fresh fruit
- 2 cups prepared plain popcorn
- 1 rice cake with 1 tablespoon peanut butter *or* jam
- assorted vegetable sticks
- 1 cup chicken *or* beef bouillon
- ¾ ounce breadsticks

Brown-Bag Lunches

Why settle for boring brown-bag lunches? Try some of our suggestions and enjoy nutritious portion-controlled lunches that taste great, too!

1 ounce sliced baked Virginia ham and 1 ounce sliced Swiss cheese
    with lettuce leaves and mustard on 2 slices rye bread
Cauliflower florets and carrot sticks
2 medium oatmeal cookies (1 ounce)

2 tablespoons whipped cream cheese and 1 tablespoon dark raisins
    on 2 slices pumpernickel bread
Celery sticks and cucumber slices
1 medium plum

2 ounces sliced roast turkey with tomato slices, alfalfa sprouts, and
    1 tablespoon Russian dressing in 1-ounce pita bread
1 medium sour pickle
1 small apple

2 ounces drained canned tuna with chopped celery and onion and
    2 teaspoons reduced-calorie mayonnaise on 2 slices whole
    wheat bread
Cherry tomatoes
1 large tangerine

2 ounces sliced liverwurst with shredded lettuce and mustard on
    2 slices rye bread
Zucchini and carrot sticks
20 small grapes

1 hard-cooked egg, sliced, with lettuce leaves and 2 teaspoons
    reduced-calorie mayonnaise on 2 slices reduced-calorie
    wheat bread
Whole mushrooms and broccoli florets
¾ ounce mixed dried fruit

2 ounces Brie cheese
¾ ounce flatbreads
Celery sticks and cucumber slices
1 small pear

2 tablespoons peanut butter and 1 tablespoon reduced-calorie grape
    spread on 2 slices raisin bread
Carrot sticks
1 small orange

Weight Watchers Metric Conversion Table

WEIGHT

To Change	To	Multiply by
Ounces	Grams	30.0
Pounds	Kilograms	0.48

VOLUME

To Change	To	Multiply by
Teaspoons	Milliliters	5.0
Tablespoons	Milliliters	15.0
Cups	Milliliters	250.0
Cups	Liters	0.25
Pints	Liters	0.5
Quarts	Liters	1.0
Gallons	Liters	4.0

LENGTH

To Change	To	Multiply by
Inches	Millimeters	25.0
Inches	Centimeters	2.5
Feet	Centimeters	30.0
Yards	Meters	0.9

TEMPERATURE

To change degrees Fahrenheit to degrees Celsius subtract 32° and multiply by ⅝.

Oven Temperatures

Degrees Fahrenheit =	Degrees Celsius	Degrees Fahrenheit =	Degrees Celsius
250	120	400	200
275	140	425	220
300	150	450	230
325	160	475	250
350	180	500	260
375	190	525	270

METRIC SYMBOLS

Symbol =	Metric Unit	Symbol =	Metric Unit
g	gram	°C	degrees Celsius
kg	kilogram	mm	millimeter
ml	milliliter	cm	centimeter
l	liter	m	meter

Dry and Liquid Measure Equivalents

Teaspoons	Tablespoons	Cups	Fluid Ounces
3 teaspoons	1 tablespoon		½ fluid ounce
6 teaspoons	2 tablespoons	⅛ cup	1 fluid ounce
12 teaspoons	4 tablespoons	¼ cup	2 fluid ounces
16 teaspoons	5 tablespoons plus 1 teaspoon	⅓ cup	
18 teaspoons	6 tablespoons	⅓ cup plus 2 teaspoons	3 fluid ounces
24 teaspoons	8 tablespoons	½ cup	4 fluid ounces
30 teaspoons	10 tablespoons	½ cup plus 2 tablespoons	5 fluid ounces
32 teaspoons	10 tablespoons plus 2 teaspoons	⅔ cup	
36 teaspoons	12 tablespoons	¾ cup	6 fluid ounces
42 teaspoons	14 tablespoons	1 cup less 2 tablespoons	7 fluid ounces
48 teaspoons	16 tablespoons	1 cup	8 fluid ounces
96 teaspoons	32 tablespoons	2 cups (1 pint)	16 fluid ounces
		4 cups (1 quart)	32 fluid ounces

Note: Measurements of less than ⅛ teaspoon are considered a dash or a pinch.

INDEX

Each recipe in this ENGAGEMENT CALENDAR is listed alphabetically, followed by the month in which it is featured. Recipes listed as *Buffet* are featured following the December recipes.

1988

JANUARY
S	M	T	W	T	F	S
					1	2
3	4	5	6	7	8	9
10	11	12	13	14	15	16
17	18	19	20	21	22	23
24/31	25	26	27	28	29	30

FEBRUARY
S	M	T	W	T	F	S
	1	2	3	4	5	6
7	8	9	10	11	12	13
14	15	16	17	18	19	20
21	22	23	24	25	26	27
28	29					

MARCH
S	M	T	W	T	F	S
		1	2	3	4	5
6	7	8	9	10	11	12
13	14	15	16	17	18	19
20	21	22	23	24	25	26
27	28	29	30	31		

APRIL
S	M	T	W	T	F	S
					1	
3	4	5	6	7	8	
10	11	12	13	14	15	
17	18	19	20	21	22	
24	25	26	27	28		

MAY
S	M	T	W	T	F	S
1	2	3	4	5	6	7
8	9	10	11	12	13	14
15	16	17	18	19	20	21
22	23	24	25	26	27	28
29	30	31				

JUNE
S	M	T	W	T	F	S
			1	2	3	4
5	6	7	8	9	10	11
12	13	14	15	16	17	18
19	20	21	22	23	24	25
26	27	28	29	30		

JULY
S	M	T	W	T	F	S
					1	2
3	4	5	6	7	8	9
10	11	12	13	14	15	16
17	18	19	20	21	22	23
24/31	25	26	27	28	29	30

AUGUST
S	M	T	W	T	F	S
	1	2	3	4	5	6
7	8	9	10	11	12	13
14	15	16	17	18	19	20
21	22	23	24	25	26	27
28	29	30	31			

SEPTEMBER
S	M	T	W	T	F	S
				1	2	3
4	5	6	7	8	9	10
11	12	13	14	15	16	17
18	19	20	21	22	23	24
25	26	27	28	29	30	

OCTOBER
S	M	T	W	T	F	S
						1
2	3	4	5	6	7	8
9	10	11	12	13	14	15
16	17	18	19	20	21	22
23/30	24/31	25	26	27	28	29

NOVEMBER
S	M	T	W	T	F	S
		1	2	3	4	5
6	7	8	9	10	11	12
13	14	15	16	17	18	19
20	21	22	23	24	25	26
27	28	29	30			

DECEMBER
S	M	T	W	T	F	S
				1	2	
4	5	6	7	8	9	
11	12	13	14	15	16	
18	19	20	21	22	23	
25	26	27	28	29	30	

1989

JANUARY
S	M	T	W	T	F	S
1	2	3	4	5	6	7
8	9	10	11	12	13	14
15	16	17	18	19	20	21
22	23	24	25	26	27	28
29	30	31				

FEBRUARY
S	M	T	W	T	F	S
			1	2	3	4
5	6	7	8	9	10	11
12	13	14	15	16	17	18
19	20	21	22	23	24	25
26	27	28				

MARCH
S	M	T	W	T	F	S
			1	2	3	4
5	6	7	8	9	10	11
12	13	14	15	16	17	18
19	20	21	22	23	24	25
26	27	28	29	30	31	

APRIL
S	M	T	W	T	F	S
						1
2	3	4	5	6	7	8
9	10	11	12	13	14	15
16	17	18	19	20	21	22
23/30	24	25	26	27	28	29

MAY
S	M	T	W	T	F	S
	1	2	3	4	5	6
7	8	9	10	11	12	13
14	15	16	17	18	19	20
21	22	23	24	25	26	27
28	29	30	31			

JUNE
S	M	T	W	T	F	S
				1	2	3
4	5	6	7	8	9	10
11	12	13	14	15	16	17
18	19	20	21	22	23	24
25	26	27	28	29	30	

JULY
S	M	T	W	T	F	S
						1
2	3	4	5	6	7	8
9	10	11	12	13	14	15
16	17	18	19	20	21	22
23/30	24/31	25	26	27	28	29

AUGUST
S	M	T	W	T	F	S
	1	2	3	4	5	
6	7	8	9	10	11	12
13	14	15	16	17	18	19
20	21	22	23	24	25	26
27	28	29	30	31		

SEPTEMBER
S	M	T	W	T	F	S
					1	2
3	4	5	6	7	8	9
10	11	12	13	14	15	16
17	18	19	20	21	22	23
24	25	26	27	28	29	30

OCTOBER
S	M	T	W	T	F	S
1	2	3	4	5	6	7
8	9	10	11	12	13	14
15	16	17	18	19	20	21
22	23	24	25	26	27	28
29	30	31				

NOVEMBER
S	M	T	W	T	F	S
			1	2	3	4
5	6	7	8	9	10	11
12	13	14	15	16	17	18
19	20	21	22	23	24	25
26	27	28	29	30		

DECEMBER
S	M	T	W	T	F	S
					1	2
3	4	5	6	7	8	9
10	11	12	13	14	15	16
17	18	19	20	21	22	23
24/31	25	26	27	28	29	30

1990

JANUARY
S	M	T	W	T	F	S
	1	2	3	4	5	6
7	8	9	10	11	12	13
14	15	16	17	18	19	20
21	22	23	24	25	26	27
28	29	30	31			

FEBRUARY
S	M	T	W	T	F	S
				1	2	3
4	5	6	7	8	9	10
11	12	13	14	15	16	17
18	19	20	21	22	23	24
25	26	27	28			

MARCH
S	M	T	W	T	F	S
				1	2	3
4	5	6	7	8	9	10
11	12	13	14	15	16	17
18	19	20	21	22	23	24
25	26	27	28	29	30	31

APRIL
S	M	T	W	T	F	S
1	2	3	4	5	6	7
8	9	10	11	12	13	
15	16	17	18	19	20	
22	23	24	25	26	27	
29	30					

MAY
S	M	T	W	T	F	S
		1	2	3	4	5
6	7	8	9	10	11	12
13	14	15	16	17	18	19
20	21	22	23	24	25	26
27	28	29	30	31		

JUNE
S	M	T	W	T	F	S
					1	2
3	4	5	6	7	8	9
10	11	12	13	14	15	16
17	18	19	20	21	22	23
24	25	26	27	28	29	30

JULY
S	M	T	W	T	F	S
1	2	3	4	5	6	7
8	9	10	11	12	13	14
15	16	17	18	19	20	21
22	23	24	25	26	27	28
29	30	31				

AUGUST
S	M	T	W	T	F	S
			1	2	3	
5	6	7	8	9	10	
12	13	14	15	16	17	
19	20	21	22	23	24	
26	27	28	29	30	31	

SEPTEMBER
S	M	T	W	T	F	S
						1
2	3	4	5	6	7	8
9	10	11	12	13	14	15
16	17	18	19	20	21	22
23/30	24	25	26	27	28	29

OCTOBER
S	M	T	W	T	F	S
	1	2	3	4	5	6
7	8	9	10	11	12	13
14	15	16	17	18	19	20
21	22	23	24	25	26	27
28	29	30	31			

NOVEMBER
S	M	T	W	T	F	S
				1	2	3
4	5	6	7	8	9	10
11	12	13	14	15	16	17
18	19	20	21	22	23	24
25	26	27	28	29	30	

DECEMBER
S	M	T	W	T	F	S
						1
2	3	4	5	6	7	
9	10	11	12	13	14	
16	17	18	19	20	21	
23/30	24/31	25	26	27	28	